SZECHWAN & NORTHERN COOKING:
FROM HOT TO COLD

BY
RHODA YEE

PUBLISHED BY TAYLOR & NG · SAN FRANCISCO · 1982

TO ALL SZECHWAN FOOD LOVERS: LET'S KEEP WOKING!

ISBN 0-912738-14-6
Library of Congress Card Number 82-50788
Printed in the United States of America
Copyright ©1982 Rhoda Yee
Published by Taylor & Ng Press
P.O. Box 200
Brisbane, California 94005
   All Rights Reserved
   First Edition, First Printing 1982
Distributed by Random House, Inc.
and in Canada by Random House of Canada Ltd.
ISBN 394-71433-4

ABOUT THE AUTHORESS

Rhoda Fong Yee was born in Canton, capital of Kwongtung Province in Southern China. A good part of her childhood was spent in Loan Gon Doan, her father's village. It was her experience during this part of her childhood which inspired Rhoda to write her fascinating cookbooks, of which **Szechwan Cooking** is her latest.

At the age of twelve, Rhoda migrated to this country and settled in Sacramento, California. She learned the basics of Chinese cuisine from her mother, who is an excellent cook, having received training from several family chefs.

In 1962, three years after graduating from U.C. Berkeley, Rhoda married Paul Yee, who coincidently shares her love and enthusiasm for Chinese food. Together they have delighted their friends with scrumptious Chinese feasts in their home in Walnut Creek.

Rhoda began to give Chinese cooking instructions fourteen years ago. Called a "master" by **Bon Appetit** magazine, she has been featured in numerous national and regional television programs, including **Good Morning America** and **Hour Magazine.** She demonstrates wok cooking across the nation for Taylor & Ng, as well as carrying a full teaching schedule.

Rhoda's other books include **Chinese Village Cookbook** and **Dim Sum.**

TABLE OF CONTENTS

PREFACE
- I SOME LIKE IT HOT 1
- II SOME LIKE IT COLD 11
- III SOME LIKE IT IN A POT 19
- VI ...NINE DAYS OLD 29
- V SOME LIKE IT RICH 39
- VI SOME LIKE IT MILD 53
- VII SOME LIKE IT SWEET AND SOUR 63
- VIII SOME LIKE IT WILD 73
- IX NEVER WOK ALONE! 77
- X GLOSSARY 86
- XI INDEX OF RECIPES 100

PREFACE

My first encounter with Szechwan food was like hosting a Chinese New Year celebration in my mouth.

I've always prided myself on my ability to eat hot spicy food and, in fact, I earned the title of "cast iron mouth" while visiting Mexico. There, every morning, I'd down Huevos Rancheros drenched in the hottest salsa with neither a tear in my eye nor a sniffle in my nose. So, knowing my capabilities, I naturally was skeptical when my friend, who grew up in the Szechwan Province, warned me not to eat the hot chili peppers. You guessed it. I took the bait hook, line, and sinker.

Gingerly. I bit into one of those dried whole chili peppers, smoky black from being fried in hot oil. Nothing happened. "This is a cinch", I thought confidently, smiling in secret delight. Little did I know these peppers have a delayed reaction. Boldly now, I chewed it a few more times and then...all of a sudden... the roof of my mouth caved in.

My tongue was jabbed by a thousand exploding firecrackers. Tears gushed forth like the great Niagara. My sinuses became wind tunnels with a hot and dry Sahara wind howling fiercely through. With every breath I saw smoke.

While my friends laughed hysterically, I begrudgingly relinquished my title of "cast iron mouth".

Well...my pride was beaten but my spirit was

unbowed. I developed a healthy respect for these peppers, along with a curiosity toward this spicy regional Chinese cuisine. I began patronizing various Szechwan and Northern Chinese restaurants while consulting the very few cookbooks available. Finally, I began cooking and experimenting on my own. Often, when I found a dish I particularly liked in a restaurant, I'd save the leftover sauce, take it home and proceed to duplicate it by trial and error. Once I went back to the same restaurant 15 times before I achieved the exact taste and texture in my own kitchen.

My good friend Hilary Miller, an excellent cook and instructor in Chinese cuisine, introduced me to her teacher, Vera Yang, a vivacious, down-to-earth woman who had just retired from being the chef/owner of her own restaurant. She showed me her methods of smoking duck, chicken and fish, and served me some of her favorite dishes, all well known to patrons of her San Francisco restaurant.

As I ate, I discovered that Szechwan cooking, as done in most restaurants or documented in most cookbooks, is quite a bit more greasy than Cantonese food. Many meat dishes are quickly deep fried in 3 to 4 cups of oil, then stir fried. I even found the amount of oil used in stir frying is greater than in Cantonese cooking. I started making changes in recipes and found I could achieve the same results without using as much oil. I've also cut down on the use of chili peppers to suit my taste which leans toward mild and medium hot.

A trip to China last year offered a wonderful opportunity to sample different styles of cooking from the country's many regions. The pungent food of the Szechwan and Hunan Provinces is marvelously balanced by delicate and smooth Northern dishes such as Velvet Chicken and Napa Cabbage In Cream Sauce. The dishes of the Shanghai region are known for rich, smooth sauces with lots of sugar and soy sauce. One of my favorites, created by a now-retired chef of the Jien Jiang Hotel in Shanghai, is a Sweet and Sour Pork so rich in sauce and robust in flavor you wouldn't believe it shared the same name with its Cantonese counterpart.

The final results are here in this little book -- my favorite Szechwan and Northern food with a few Cantonese dishes included here and there. The latter are family recipes I didn't have space for in my first book, **The Chinese Village Cookbook.**

I hope you'll enjoy preparing and eating these dishes. To enhance your dinner, include a glass of beer, chilled sparkling cider, or white wine and, by all means, a glass of ice water. You'll be well on your way to adding "a little spice to your life".

SOME LIKE IT HOT

Szechwan Province is located in the Western part of China where the summers are very hot. The two most obvious reasons why the people use chili peppers in their cooking are because it does a good job of ventilating their systems (how well I know it), and because it stimulates the appetite (but only if your taste buds are still in operation).

For whatever reasons, Szechwanese use chili peppers in many forms -- fresh, dried, minced or crushed. In addition, many hot chili sauces and pastes are available in cans and jars. A favorite table condiment and seasoning agent is hot chili oil. Many brands are available here but it's easy to make your own.

HOT CHILI OIL WITH GARLIC

Yield: ¾ cup

1 cup oil
½ cup dried chili peppers, finely chopped
1 tbsp. sesame seeds
8-10 cloves garlic, crushed
2 tbsp. water
Handfull of Szechwan peppercorns

Preparation: Mix chopped chili peppers with sesame seeds, crushed garlic and water in an oven-proof bowl.

Cooking: Heat oil in a small sauce pan. Test oil by dropping in a handful of Szechwan peppercorns. Oil should not be so hot that they burn. Now pour the hot oil over the chili mixture. Cool for 8 hours and strain off the oil.

Comments: This makes a delightful hostess gift for someone smitten with Szechwan cooking. The crushed garlic adds a tantalizing aroma and distinctive flavor to the chili oil.

This next dish is my favorite shrimp recipe from a well-known Northern Chinese restaurant in Albany, California. No other restaurant fixes shrimp quite like this. I brought home the leftover sauce each time I ate there and after umpteen times of trial and error, to say nothing of running back to the restaurant for more of the same, I finally managed to create the right combination of seasonings. On a scale of 1 to 10, I'd modestly rate this an 11. It's so good you'll lick the last drop of sauce off the plate.

SPICY SHRIMP

Yield: Serves 6 to 8

½ lb. medium size raw shrimp
Batter:
  1 medium egg
  2 tbsp. water
  6-8 tbsp. cornstarch
Sauce mixture:
  4 tbsp. Kikkoman soy sauce
  4 tbsp. water
  4 tbsp. sugar
  2 tbsp. rice vinegar
  1 tbsp. sherry
  1 tbsp. sesame oil
  ¼-½ tsp. dried chili pepper, crushed
  2 tbsp. garlic, thinly sliced
  1 tbsp. fresh ginger, minced
  2 tbsp. green onions, minced
  3 cups oil for deep frying

Preparation: Shell, clean and devein shrimp. Sprinkle lightly with salt and add to batter. Combine sauce ingredients.

Cooking: In wok, heat oil until hot. Drop in shrimp, one by one. Deep fry 8 to 10 at a time for 18 to 20 seconds. Batter should be a light golden color. Drain well. Place on platter. Pour off oil and add sauce mixture to the wok. Reduce mixture for about 2 minutes. Pour sauce over shrimp and garnish with green onions.

Do-Ahead Notes: Deep fry shrimp and mix sauce ingredients 4 to 6 hours ahead of time. Just before serving, deep fry shrimp a second time in one wok while cooking the sauce mixture in another. Combine shrimp and sauce and serve.

Comments: The amount of cornstarch in the batter varies with the size of the egg. Just make sure it isn't too thick or thin. If it's too thin, the batter won't cling to the shrimp. This batter is delicate and, if the proportions are proper, it will have a translucent quality. You should be able to see the shrimp through the batter. Do not, I repeat, do not reheat the shrimp in the oven as that will toughen them. The second frying is done briefly, just enough to crisp the batter and reheat the shrimp. Fry the second time only 12 to 15 seconds in *very* hot oil.

THE FAMOUS 3 A.M. SNACK

"Kung Po" means guardian of the throne. Way back when, a legend says, there was a general who was one of the throne's guardians. He was a huge man with an appetite to match. He had his own personal chef travelling with him at all times and whenever he became hungry (even in the midst of battle), he'd order his chef to fix him a little snack. That "little" snack was enough to feed an entire football squad.

One night he woke up thoroughly famished and commanded his chef to prepare another of his famous snacks. Unfortunately for the chef, the general had finished another snack just 3 hours earlier and all the provisions for the day had been eaten. Panic-stricken, the chef searched the kitchen for anything edible; finally finding some leftover chicken and a few bell peppers. "What else can I add to make this small amount of food enough for the general!", he mumbled to himself. Luckily he found some raw peanuts in the cupboard. Since the freshness of the chicken was questionable, the chef decided he'd add lots of dried chili peppers to hide the stale flavor of the meat. Well, the general loved the hot and spicy concoction (at 3 a.m. I really wonder if he knew what he'd eaten) and promptly named it after the position he held. Thus, the birth of the now famous "Kung Po Chicken".

KUNG PO CHICKEN

Yield: Serves 4

4 chicken thighs, boned and cut into small cubes
Meat marinade:
  2 tsp. cornstarch
  1 tsp. sesame oil
  1 tsp. sherry
  1 tsp. Kikkoman soy sauce

1 small green pepper, seeded and cut into
　　small cubes
⅔ cup raw, shelled peanuts
1 tbsp. garlic, minced
3-4 dried chili peppers
Sauce mixture:
　　1 tsp. hoisin sauce
　　1 tsp. hot bean sauce
　　1 tsp. Kikkoman soy sauce
　　1 tsp. sherry
　　½ tsp. rice vinegar
　　½ tsp. sesame oil
　　¼ tsp. sugar
⅓ cup oil

Preparation: Combine sauce ingredients. Pour marinade over chicken and mix well.

Cooking: Heat wok until hot. Add ⅓ cup oil and heat to medium hot. Fry peanuts until golden. Remove peanuts with bamboo strainer and, in the same oil, stir fry the green pepper for 1 minute. Set aside. Add whole chili peppers and, when they turn black, add chicken pieces and minced garlic. Stir fry until chicken becomes firm. Add sauce mixture and stir until well thickened. Add vegetables and peanuts. Mix well.

Do-Ahead Notes: Do through preparation early in the day.

Comments: A dish with "Kung Po" or "Kung Pao" in its name must include whole dry chili peppers cooked to a crisp black and, most likely, peanuts will also be found in it. The flavor is usually fairly hot. To make it milder, decrease the number of whole dry chili peppers and use less hot bean sauce. This recipe is mild compared to those served in most restaurants.

MONGOLIAN BEEF

Yield: Serves 6 to 8

¾ lb. flank steak
Meat marinade:
　　1-2 egg whites, lightly beaten
　　1 tbsp. cornstarch
　　2 tsp. oil
　　1 tsp. sherry
　　½ tsp. salt
　　A few dashes white pepper
Sauce mixture:
　　4 tbsp. Kikkoman soy sauce
　　1½ tbsp. sugar
　　1 tbsp. dark soy sauce
　　1 tbsp. sesame oil
　　1 tbsp. sherry
　　1 tsp. white vinegar
　　½ tsp. hot bean sauce
　　½ tsp. sweet bean sauce
　　½-1 tsp. dried chili pepper, crushed
　　2-3 tbsp. garlic, minced
½ oz. bean thread
6 large green onions, cut into 1-inch lengths
3-5 dried chili peppers
2 cups oil
1 tsp. cornstarch mixed with 2 tsp. water

Preparation: Cut flank steak cross-grain into ⅛-inch slices. Mix with meat marinade. Combine sauce ingredients.

Cooking: In wok, heat 1½ cups oil to very hot. Deep fry bean threads (they will puff up instantly). Set bean threads aside. Add the remaining ½ cup oil (this is to cool down the oil already in the wok). Make sure it is now no hotter than 250°. To test, place a piece of beef in the oil. It should just **barely** sizzle. Deep fry beef in two separate batches until just done, about 10 seconds. Drain off all but 2 tbsp. oil. Pour in sauce mixture and let it reduce for 2 minutes over high heat. Add green onions, stirring for 15 seconds. Add beef and stir until well mixed. If the sauce appears a bit thin, add a little of the cornstarch/water mixture to thicken. Place beef on top of bean threads and serve.

Comments: This is a wonderfully rich and velvety dish. The beef is cooked by the velveting method (see page 54) and, if done properly, will melt in your mouth. I tried stir frying the beef instead of using the velveting method and it didn't have the same texture.

If you have two woks, cook the sauce in one while cooking the beef in the other. It'll go much faster. If the taste is too hot, decrease chili peppers.

SPICY BEAN CAKES

Yield: Serves 4
- 2 cakes very soft bean cake (tofu)
- ¼ cup ground pork
- Sauce mixture:
  - 2 tbsp. hot bean sauce
  - 2 tbsp. sweet bean sauce
  - 1 tbsp. Kikkoman soy sauce
  - 2 tbsp. water
  - 1 tsp. rice vinegar
- 1½-2 tbsp. oil
- 2 tbsp. garlic, minced
- ½ tsp. Szechwan peppercorns, ground
- 2 tbsp. green onions, minced
- 1 tsp. cornstarch mixed with 2 tsp. water

Preparation: Cut bean cakes into ¾-inch cubes. Bring 1 quart water to boil. Add bean cakes. When the water begins to simmer, drain. Combine sauce ingredients.

Cooking: Heat wok until hot. Add oil, minced garlic and Szechwan peppercorn. After a few seconds, add ground pork. Stir fry until done. Add sauce mixture, then the bean cakes. Gently toss bean cakes to coat with sauce mixture. Cook until bean cakes are heated through, about 1-2 minutes. If necessary, add enough of the cornstarch/water mixture to thicken sauce. Mix with green onions and serve.

Do-Ahead Notes: Do through preparation several hours in advance.

Comments: There are many kinds of bean cakes. Chinese and Japanese bean cakes differ in firmness and texture. The most common Chinese bean cake

(dow fu) has a firm texture and the cakes are smaller, usually 4-inches by 4-inches by 1-inch. The Japanese version called tofu or tufu is softer and ususally is sold in one big block, about 4-inches by 4-inches by 4-inches. For this recipe, buy the softest Japanese kind called Kinugoshi. It has a smooth appearance and the texture is much like custard. To firm it, parboil as directed in the preparation phase. If you can't find the soft tofu, use the Chinese kind but eliminate the parboiling step. Later on, in other recipes, we'll be using Chinese bean cakes.

THE PURPLE JEWEL

Eggplant is one of my favorite vegetables. Its unusual coloring, delicate texture and absorbancy lends itself perfectly to spicy Szechwan seasonings. The Oriental eggplant is small and looks like a blackjack. It's sweeter, tastier and cooks faster than the Western variety, although either can be used in the following recipes. Generally, cook the Western eggplant a little longer.

EGGPLANT SZECHWAN

Yield: Serves 4 to 6

5 Oriental eggplants (or 1 large Western eggplant, about 1-1½ lbs.)
1-2 tsp. dried chili pepper, crushed
2 tbsp. garlic, minced
3 large green onions, cut into 1-inch lengths
Sauce mixture:
  ¼ cup Kikkoman soy sauce
  ¼ cup water
  ¼ tsp. white pepper
  1 tsp. sugar
  ½ tsp. rice vinegar
  2 tsp. cornstarch
⅓ cup oil

Preparation: Cut eggplant into 3-inch by 1-inch pieces. Cover with ice water and refrigerate for 1 hour. Drain well and pat dry with paper towels. Leave in refrigerator until ready to use. Combine sauce ingredients.

Cooking: In wok, heat ⅓ cup of oil until smoking. Add eggplant and toss until well coated with oil. Salt lightly and cover for 2 minutes. Uncover and cook another minute. If eggplant looks dry, add a little water. Add garlic and chili pepper and continue cooking until eggplant is tender. Add green onions, then the sauce mixture. Stir until sauce thickens.

Do-Ahead Notes: This dish will keep nicely in a warm oven for 10 to 15 minutes.

Comments: This rich and full-bodied dish is my friend Hilary Miller's recipe. Soaking the eggplant in ice water firms the texture and closes pores so there is less oil absorption during cooking.

EGGPLANT SZECHWAN WITH PORK

Yield: Serves 4

4 small Oriental eggplants (or 1 Western eggplant, no larger than 1 lb.)
½ cup ground pork (about 3 oz.)
2 tbsp. oil
3-4 whole dried chili peppers
2 tbsp. garlic, minced
½ cup chicken broth
Sauce mixture:
  1 tbsp. bean sauce
  1 tbsp. hot bean sauce
  3 tbsp. Kikkoman soy sauce
  3 tbsp. water
  1 tsp. sesame oil
  2 tsp. sugar
  2 tsp. rice vinegar
  2 tsp. cornstarch
1 green onion, minced

Preparation: Cube eggplant into 1½-inch pieces. Combine sauce ingredients.

Cooking: In wok, heat oil with whole chili peppers and garlic. Add pork when garlic starts turning beige. Cook until pork is done, about 1 to 1½ minutes. Add eggplant pieces and chicken broth. Cover and simmer 3 minutes until eggplant is tender (longer for the Western variety). Add more broth if necessary. Add sauce mixture and stir until thickened. Add green onion.

Do-Ahead Notes: Do through preparation early in the day.

Comments: This recipe uses the least amount of oil, a mere 2 tbsp. instead of ⅓ cup or more. All these eggplant recipes are good and have different seasonings and cooking methods. Try them all before deciding on a favorite.

YU HSIANG EGGPLANT

Yield: Serves 4 to 6

    6 small Oriental eggplants (or 1 large Western eggplant, about 1-1½ lbs.)
    3 small fresh green chili peppers, coarsely chopped
    2 tbsp. garlic, coarsely chopped
    Sauce mixture:
        1 tbsp. Kikkoman soy sauce
        ½ tsp. salt
        ½ tsp. sesame oil
        2 tbsp. water
        2 tsp. sugar
        1 tsp. cornstarch
    2 tbsp. green onions, coarsely chopped
    2 cups oil

Preparation: Cut eggplant into 3-inch by 1-inch pieces. Combine sauce ingredients.

Cooking: In wok, heat oil until hot. Deep fry eggplant until golden brown, about 4-5 minutes. Drain well on paper towels. Pour off all but 1 tbsp. oil. Add chopped chili peppers and garlic, then eggplant pieces. Add sauce mixture. Toss to coat well. Add green onions and serve.

Do-Ahead Notes: Deep fry eggplant early in the day and combine sauce ingredients.

Comments: The small green chili pepper used here is the Serrano variety. As a general rule, the smaller the chili pepper, the hotter it is. But even though the chili is hot, the dish itself is relatively mild because of the eggplant's absorbing capacity. The term "Yu Hsiang" means "fish fragrance" and applies to any dish using lots of garlic, green onion and/or fresh ginger; the same ingredients used in many fish dishes. This recipe is a fairly mild version without ginger.

ANTS CLIMBING THE TREE

What a lively imagination the Chinese have! This popular Szechwan dish is known as "Ants Climbing The Tree." The bean threads, turned a reddish-brown by the sauce, resemble tree bark and the minced pork looks like ants. I'm sure the reason is obvious why I've renamed this dish:

SPICY BEAN THREADS WITH MINCED PORK

Yield: Serves 4

    4 oz. bean threads
    1 cup ground pork (about 6-7 oz.)
    1 tbsp. Kikkoman soy sauce
    1 tbsp. hot bean sauce
    2 tsp. ground bean sauce
    1 tbsp. dark soy sauce
    ¾ cup chicken broth
    2 tbsp. green onions, chopped
    2 tbsp. oil

Preparation: Pour 4 cups boiling water over bean threads and soak for ½ hour. Drain and set aside.

Cooking: In wok, heat oil and stir fry ground pork until done. Add soy sauce, hot bean sauce and ground bean sauce. Mix well. Add bean threads and chicken broth. Stir to mix well. Let ingredients cook until all or most of the broth evaporates. Add green onions. Mix and serve.

Do-Ahead Notes: A great dish to make ahead early in the day. To reheat, add a little broth and reheat on top of stove on low heat.

BRAISED FISH WITH HOT BEAN SAUCE

Yield: Serves 4

    1 whole 1½-2 lb. rock cod or red snapper
    Sauce mixture:
        3 tbsp. fresh ginger, minced
        1½ tbsp. garlic, minced
        1 tbsp. hot bean sauce
        4 tbsp. Kikkoman soy sauce
        2 tbsp. sugar
        1 cup water
    ¼ cup green onions, coarsely chopped
    1 tbsp. cornstarch mixed with 2 tbsp. water
    3 cups oil

Preparation: After the fish has been cleaned and scaled, make 4 deep vertical scores on each side. Combine sauce ingredients.

Cooking: In 3 cups oil, deep fry each side of the fish for 5 to 6 minutes or until just done. Drain on paper towel. Pour off all but 2 tbsp. oil. Add sauce mixture and place fish back in wok. Simmer for 5 minutes, uncovered. Add green onions. Add cornstarch/water mixture to thicken sauce. Serve.

Do-Ahead Notes: Fish can be deep fried ahead and kept 2 to 3 hours in the refrigerator. Finish cooking it in the sauce just before serving.

Comments: You'll love this fish. There are many kinds of hot bean sauce, red chili sauce or hot chili sauces available in Chinese grocery stores. Generally, sauces in cans are slightly milder than those in jars. Try several brands to determine which you prefer.

SOME LIKE IT COLD

There's nothing more refreshing on a hot summer day than a cold salad or main dish. Cold dishes are rare in Chinese cooking because refrigeration is scarce. That's why it's such a treat for me to share some of my favorite chilled dishes with you. Some are spicy, others aren't. But they're all delicious and excellent for make-ahead meals.

Chickens in China, unless they were raised in a cage, are much tougher than those found in the United States, since most are allowed to run free in the villages. They aren't as plump, and they're older because the hens are saved to lay eggs. And the roosters...well...we *know* what they had to do. Be that as it may, the term "Pan Pan" is the sound produced by peasants who had to pound the chicken breasts to tenderize them.

PAN PAN CHICKEN

Yield: Serves 4 to 6

1½ chicken breasts
1 medium sized cucumber, about 5 to 6-inches long
Sauce mixture:
 1 tbsp. peanut butter
 1½ tbsp. Kikkoman soy sauce
 ½ tbsp. Worcheshire sauce
 2 tsp. sesame oil
 2 tsp. hot chili oil
 2 tsp. sugar
 1 tbsp. black or rice vinegar
 ½ tsp. light soy sauce
 1 tsp. fresh lemon juice
 ½ tsp. dried chili pepper, crushed
 2 tbsp. garlic, minced
 1 tbsp. fresh ginger, minced

Preparation: Peel and seed cucumber. Cut into 2-inch long thin strips. Salt chicken breasts and steam for 12 to 15 minutes, starting to time after water comes to a boil. Cool. Discard bones and skin. Cut chicken into thin strips. Combine sauce ingredients.

Assembling: Place cucumber strips on a plate and top with chicken. Pour sauce over top. Garnish with Chinese parsley or other fresh greens such as watercress or regular parsley. Top with tomato rose.

Do-Ahead Notes: Assemble everything on plate several hours in advance. Withhold sauce until serving time.

Comments: In China, sesame paste is used instead of peanut butter. In this country, however, peanut butter makes a good substitute unless you live close to a Chinatown and have access to sesame paste. Another substitute even better than peanut butter, is a peanut-based barbecue sauce called "Boemboe Sate", usually available in specialty food stores. The chilled and crunchy cucumber acts as a counterbalance to the hot and spicy chicken. It's a wonderful taste sensation.

Don't let the peanut butter in the sauce turn you off. When it's mixed in, you won't even know it's there. All you'll taste is this marvelous, rich and subtly spiced sauce.

TOMATO ROSE GARNISH

Here's how to make the Tomato Rose Garnish as seen in the Pan Pan Chicken photo on page 10. It's simple to do, and adds color and flourish to any dish.

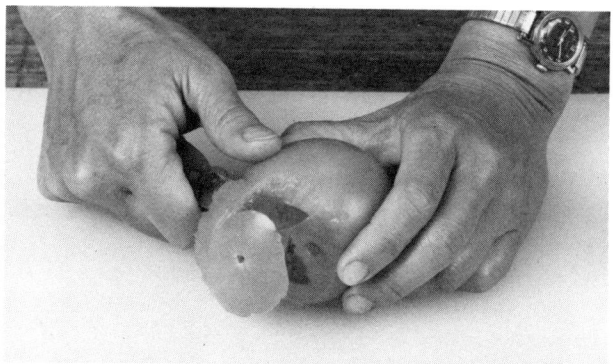

Step One: Start cutting at the base of the tomato.

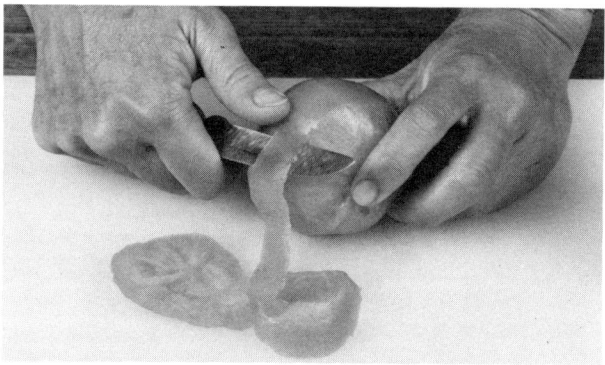

Step Two: Keep peeling in one continuous strip until the whole tomato is peeled.

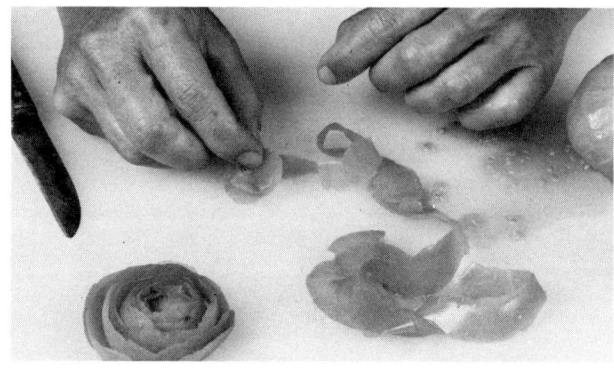

Step Three: Start coiling up the tomato skin inside out.

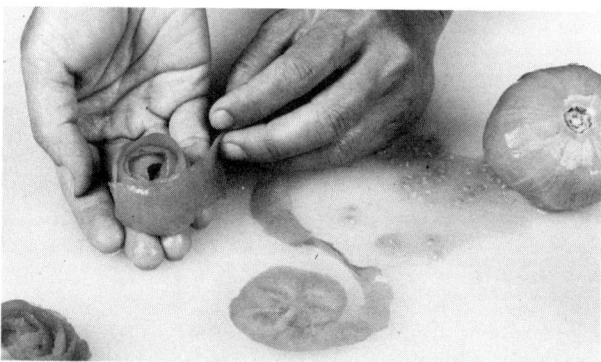

Step Four: Continue winding the peeled skin until you get to the base. Then set aside the coil on top of the base. Voila! There is your rose!

CHINESE SPINACH SALAD WITH FRESH WATER CHESTNUTS

Yield: Serves 4 to 6

    2 bunches young, tender spinach
    12 fresh water chestnuts, peeled and thinly sliced
    One 8-oz. can mandarin oranges
    Dressing:
        Same as for rainbow salad

Preparation: Wash spinach. Drain well. Break larger leaves into smaller pieces. Drain juice from mandarin oranges.

Assembling: Place ingredients into a salad bowl. Add dressing and toss.

Comments: Fresh water chestnuts have a deep brown skin and resemble flower bulbs. Since they grow in muddy water, they're often caked with dried mud. Once the outer skin is peeled, you can eat them raw or add them to soups and stir fried dishes. Fresh water chestnuts have a sweet flavor and crunchy texture similar to a coconut's. Canned water chestnuts have no flavor whatsoever and even the texture isn't the same. Once you've tasted them fresh, you'll be spoiled forever. When selecting them, make sure they're hard and firm. If they feel the slightest bit soft or spongy, they're on their way out. Jicama is an excellent substitute.

RAINBOW SALAD

Yield: Serves 8 to 10

    1 small head iceberg lettuce
    ½ lb. cooked small shrimp
    1 medium carrot
    2-3 green onions, shredded into 1-inch lengths
    1 cup Chinese parsley, cut into 1-inch lengths
    Dressing:
        4 tbsp. fresh lemon juice
        2 tbsp. white vinegar
        4 tbsp. sugar
        4 tsp. light soy sauce
        4 tsp. sesame oil
        3 tbsp. salad oil
        ¾ tsp. salt
        ½ tsp. pepper

Preparation: Shred lettuce and cut carrots the size of match sticks. Mix salad dressing. Blot cooked shrimp with paper towels to make sure thay aren't watery.

Assembling: On a round or oval serving platter or in a shallow, wide glass bowl, start with 1 layer shredded lettuce, then shrimp, green onions, carrots and Chinese parsley. Repeat layering twice again, Spoon dressing over salad and serve.

Do-Ahead Notes: Do through assembling except for adding the dressing. Keeps overnight in the refrigerator.

Comments: This is a terrific recipe for make-ahead salads. It's from the Yee household, and we've been making it for years. It's so good I hope you'll try it.

CHILLED BRAISED BAMBOO SHOOTS

Yield: Serves 4 to 6

    One 8 oz. can whole bamboo shoots
    ½ cup red bell pepper, cut the size of matchsticks
    3 tbsp. oil
    Sauce mixture:
        ¼ cup chicken stock
        1 tbsp. light soy sauce
        1½ tbsp. sugar
        1 tbsp. white vinegar
        1 tsp. hot bean sauce
        1 tsp. sesame oil
        1 tsp. hot chili oil with garlic

Preparation: Cut bamboo shoots into strips about

1½-inch or 2-inches long. Combine sauce ingredients.

Cooking: In wok, heat 3 tbsp. oil until hot. Add bamboo shoots and red bell pepper. Stir fry for 1 minute and add sauce. Mix well and cover. Cook over medium heat until most of the liquid evaporates. Turn into serving dish and cool. Chill for several hours or overnight before serving.

Do-Ahead Notes: This is a perfect recipe for a working hostess. The bamboo shoots will taste much better after they've absorbed all the flavor from the sauce. This keeps well under refrigeration for several days.

SPICY CHICKEN SALAD

Yield: Serves 6 to 8
 1 whole chicken breast
 Meat marinade:
  1 tbsp. Kikkoman soy sauce
  1 tbsp. hoisin sauce
  1 tbsp. bean sauce
  1 tbsp. garlic, minced
  1 tsp. sugar
 1 oz. bean threads
 ½ head iceberg lettuce, cut into fine strips
 2 green onions, cut into 1-inch strips
 ½ bunch Chinese parsley, washed and cut into 1½-inch lengths
 ½ cup roasted peanuts, chopped
 Dressing:
  2 tbsp. oil
  2 tbsp. sesame oil
  2 tbsp. white vinegar
  2 tbsp. sugar
  2 tbsp. light soy sauce
  1 tbsp. hoisin sauce
  1 tsp. chili oil
  ½ tsp. dried chili pepper, crushed
  2 tbsp. garlic, minced

Preparation: Marinate chicken for 8 hours and bake at 375° for 35 minutes. Cool. Debone. Cut meat with skin into thin strips. Deep fry bean threads in hot oil (They'll puff up instantly). Keep bean threads in airtight container for up to 4 hours until ready to use. Mix salad dressing.

Assembling: Mix all vegetables and sliced chicken with the dressing. Add ¾ of the peanuts and most of the bean threads. Transfer to a large serving platter. Top with remaining bean threads and peanuts.

Do-Ahead Notes: Do through preparation up to 4 hours before serving.

Comments: Bean threads must be fried in very hot oil since they puff up in a second and must be cooked through in that instant. If the oil is not hot enough, the bean threads still may puff up but the interiors won't be cooked. This is a wonderfully delicious salad. Always serve Chinese salads on a platter. It shows off their beauty to more advantage than a bowl does.

THE MASTER SAUCE

A long time ago, Chinese legend tells us, a wedding was about to take place. It was traditional for the bride to bring along whatever in the way of household furnishings the family could afford as a trousseau. Alas, in this case the girl's family was extremely poor and she had nothing worthwhile in monetary terms to bring to her new husband. Her parents were saddened because they knew she would lose face if she didn't bring anything of value. After many discussions, they finally decided to give their "Master Sauce", a secret sauce that had been in the family for many years, and was used for cooking chicken, pork, and other meats on special occasions. Because the mother was known for her superb cooking, this sauce was particularly good.

When the bride settled down to her household duties, she made her first dinner for her husband's family using the Master Sauce. Everyone, especially her new mother-in-law, was impressed with her cooking skills. News travelled back to her family's village and, from then on, it was not uncommon for brides to bring their mother's precious Master Sauce as part of the trousseau.

The next three recipes are made with the Master Sauce. The cooking proceedure is the same for all, but the end result, because of the different meats used, will be quite different.

ANISE PORK

Yield: Serves 4 to 6

1-1½ lb. pork butt
Master Sauce:
 ¼ cup oil
 ⅔ cup sugar
 3 dried tangerine peels
 3 star anise
 6 large cloves garlic, mashed
 2 cups Kikkoman soy sauce
 4 cups water

Preparation: Slice pork into long strips no more than 1-inch thick.

Cooking: In a 4-5 qt. pot, heat oil and sugar together until it becomes golden. Mix remaining Master Sauce ingredients and add to carmelized sugar. Bring sauce to a boil, then turn down heat to simmer. Add pork, cover and simmer for 40 minutes. Cool. Remove meat and reserve sauce. Thinly slice pork strips and serve chilled.

Do-Ahead Notes: This recipe can be made several days in advance. However, don't slice the cooked pork strips until 1 hour before serving time to insure the meat remains moist.

Comments: The Master Sauce can be used again and again. Refrigerate between each use. If you don't use the sauce for 2 weeks, boil it briefly to renew it. It also can be frozen. As the sauce reduces, it can be returned to its original flavor by adding the necessary ingredients in proportionate amounts.

CHILLED BEEF SHANK

Yield: Serves 4 to 6

2 beef shanks, about 1 to 1½ lbs. each
1 Master Sauce recipe (page 15)

Preparation: Place sauce and beef shanks into a deep pot. Bring to a boil. Cover and simmer for 2½ to 3 hours or until tender. Turn shanks over every ½ hour to insure even coloring. Remove beef shanks and cool on a platter. Cut into thin slices. Ladle small amounts of sauce over beef slices. Cover with plastic wrap and chill before serving.

Do-Ahead Notes: Make this a day or two ahead and let the sauce soak in.

Comments: Beef shank is a tough cut of meat because it's composed of muscle with lots of connective tissue tapering off into tendons. When cooked for a long time, however, it becomes tender and the tissues have a gelatinous and chewy texture. This can be cooked in a pressure cooker for 20 minutes on medium-high heat. It makes wonderful hors d'oeuvres.

RED COOK TRIPE

Yield: Serves 4

1 lb. tripe
1 Master Sauce recipe (page 15)

Preparation: Rub tripe with salt, then with white vinegar. Bring a pot of water to a boil, add tripe and boil for 5 minutes. Discard water. Rub tripe again with salt and discard any extraneous membrane. Rinse well.

Cooking: Place tripe in a deep pot and add the Master Sauce. Bring to a boil, cover and simmer for 3 hours or until tender. Cool on platter and cut into thin slices. Reserve sauce. Serve chilled as hors d'oeuvres.

Do-Ahead Notes: Make it a day in advance.

Comments: Use the sliced tripe in stir fried dishes combining it with seasonal vegetables.

BEAN CAKE SALAD

Yield: Serves 4

2 small cakes of Chinese bean cake
⅓ cup ham, finely diced
⅓ cup celery, finely diced
⅓ cup green onions, minced
⅓ cup Chinese pickled vegetables, minced
Iceberg lettuce leaves
Dressing:
   3 tbsp. light soy sauce
   1 tbsp. rice vinegar
   2 tsp. sesame oil
   ½ tsp. sugar
   1 tbsp. sesame seeds, toasted

Preparation: Drain bean cakes well. Cut into ¼-inch cubes. Mix dressing.

Assembling: Line individual salad plates with lettuce. Mix bean cakes with ham, celery, pickled vegetables, and green onions. Toss gently with salad

dressing. Spoon equal portions onto lettuce leaves. Sprinkle with toasted sesame seeds.

Do-Ahead Notes: Do through mixing the dressing into the bean cake mixture several hours in advance.

Comments: This is a great summer salad because it's so light. It's good for someone "on the go". Just make up a large batch to last for several days. If you're a vegetarian, substitute carrots or red bell peppers for the ham. A quick word about the bean cake: it's low calorie, and because it's so easily digested, it makes a good baby food.

SPICY CUCUMBERS

Yield: Serves 6 to 8

    4 large cucumbers, about 7 to 8 inches long
    1 tsp. salt
    Sauce mixture:
        2 tbsp. Kikkoman soy sauce
        1½ tbsp. white vinegar
        1 tbsp. sesame oil
        1 tbsp. oil
        1 tbsp. sherry
        1 tbsp. hot bean sauce
        1 tbsp. sugar
        3 cloves garlic, thinly sliced

Preparation: Seed and cut cucumbers into 3-inch by ½-inch strips. Sprinkle with salt. Place in a bowl and top with a heavy object such as a smaller bowl filled with water. Let stand for 2 to 3 hours. Drain. Squeeze as much moisture as possible from cucumbers. Return to bowl and toss with sauce. Let stand 4 hours or refrigerate overnight. Serve chilled as a side dish.

Do-Ahead Notes: Make this 2 or 3 days in advance so the flavor really soaks in.

Comments: Cucumbers are sometimes bitter. Be sure to taste a small strip before making the entire recipe. To make this even hotter, add 1 tbsp. or more hot chili oil and...WOW...you'll blast off into space!

SOME LIKE IT IN A POT

Casserole cooking is universal. Even in Chinese cuisine, known best for its quick stir-fry technique, one finds casseroles. They're used in all parts of the country, especially in family-style cooking.

Special clay cooking pots made in China can usually be found in Chinatown stores. They have a rough, sandy, light beige exterior and a smoothly glazed chocolate brown interior. Fragile, they sit within a network of wires for protection.

These pots come in several shapes. The most common has a flat bottom with high, flaring sides (much like a deep pie dish), and a hollow handle on one side. A less common shape resembles a vertical watermelon with the top and bottom flattened. Each comes with a cover. The "watermelon" is used for brewing soups or thick rice congee while the former is used for most casserole dishes.

To test whether the pot is cook-worthy, ask the salesperson to fill it with water and set it on a dry surface. If the surface becomes wet, there's a leak somewhere. Or, you can float the pot in a basin of water. If water seeps into the pot, that's a reject too. Soak your clay pot in water for 24 hours before using. Remember the two paramount rules in clay pot cooking:

- Always have liquid in the pot.
- Never set a hot pot in cold water. The sudden change of temperature will cause it to crack.

Is it necessary to have a clay pot in order to make Chinese casseroles? No! Any good heat-proof casserole dish or heavy-bottomed 3 to 4-quart pot will do. Of course, the food will look more authentic served in a Chinese clay pot, but as far as taste is concerned, there's no appreciable difference.

We've already discussed some casserole recipes in the "Master Sauce" section. This chapter will give you more casserole or clay pot recipes using a wide range of meat, vegetables and seasonings. After trying a few, you can invent your own combinations. They're excellent do-ahead dishes.

CURRIED CHICKEN WITH VEGETABLES

Yield: Serves 4 to 6

One 3 lb. fryer
2 medium white potatoes
4 medium carrots
½ cup raw peanuts
1 chunk ginger, size of a quarter, crushed
3-4 cloves garlic, crushed
2 tbsp. oil
2 tsp. salt
2 tbsp. curry powder
1 tbsp. brown sugar
3 tbsp. sherry
¾ cup chicken broth
3 tbsp. catsup
⅓ cup raisins
2 green onions, cut into 1-inch lengths

Preparation: Disjoint chicken and cut into 2-inch pieces, bones and all. Peel and cut potatoes and carrots into 1-inch chunks.

Cooking: In a heavy-bottomed 4 to 5-quart pot, heat oil with crushed ginger and garlic; then brown chicken pieces evenly on all sides. Add all ingredients except raisins. Cover and simmer for ½ hour. Add raisins and cook for 15 minutes more. Add green onions during the last 5 minutes of cooking.

Do-Ahead Notes: Cook early in the day. Chicken and vegetables taste better after several hours in the sauce.

Comments: If you use a Chinese clay pot, brown chicken pieces in a wok first, then transfer them to the clay pot for the remainder of the cooking. Make sure there is adequate liquid in the pot at all times.

OXTAIL AND CHINESE TURNIP STEW

Yield: Serves 4 to 6

- 2½ lb. oxtails
- 2½-3 lb. Chinese white turnips or Japanese daikon
- 1 star anise
- 1 chunk fresh ginger, size of a brussel sprout, crushed
- 3-4 cloves garlic, crushed
- 2-3 cups beef broth
- 2 tbsp. dark soy sauce
- ½ cup water
- 2 tsp. cornstarch mixed with 3 tsp. water
- 1 tbsp. oil

Preparation: Peel turnips and cut into chunks about the same size as the oxtails (about 2-inch pieces).

Cooking: In a 4 to 5-quart pot, brown oxtails with the oil, ginger and garlic. Add 1½ cups beef broth, water, soy sauce, star anise and turnips. Cover.

Simmer for 2½ to 3 hours on medium low heat or until oxtails are tender. Check liquid. You may need to add more beef broth or water. When oxtails are done, there should be about ½ to ⅓ cup liquid left. Add the cornstarch/water mixture to thicken sauce.

Do-Ahead Notes: Make ahead and reheat. This tastes just as good, if not better, a few hours later or the next day.

Comments: You can buy these turnips, called "lo-bak" in Chinese, in a Chinatown or your own supermarket. They're sometimes called "daikon", the Japanese name. They're juicy and tasty, the oxtail is tender and succulent, and the star anise adds piquancy to the stew. If you cook this in a clay pot, be sure to brown the oxtails in a wok first, then do the simmering in the clay pot.

Try to buy the small to medium sized oxtail pieces, since the large ones are difficult to manage with chopsticks. Besides, they're not as pleasing to the eye and take longer to cook.

BRAISED MUSHROOMS IN OYSTER SAUCE

Yield: Serves 4 to 6

- 24 dried Oriental mushrooms
- One 8 oz. can peeled straw mushrooms
- One 4 oz. can button mushrooms
- One 4 oz. can baby corn
- 3-4 cloves garlic, mashed
- 1 chunk ginger, size of a quarter, mashed
- 3 tbsp. rendered chicken fat
- ½ cup chicken broth
- 2 tbsp. dark soy sauce
- 2 tbsp. oyster sauce
- 2 tsp. cornstarch mixed with 3 tsp. water
- 2 green onions, cut into 1-inch lengths

Preparation: Soak dried mushrooms for 1 hour in just enough water to cover. Squeeze dry. Reserve liquid and discard stems. Drain liquid from the canned ingredients.

Cooking: In a 2-quart pot, heat chicken fat with mashed ginger and garlic. Brown for 1 to 2 minutes. Add all the mushrooms, baby corn, ½ cup water from the soaked mushrooms, ½ cup chicken broth and dark soy sauce. Cover and simmer for ½ hour or until half the liquid is left. Add the cornstarch/water mixture and oyster sauce. Stir to thicken. Add green onions. Mix well. Salt to taste, if necessary. Serve.

Do-Ahead Notes: Make a day ahead and reheat on low burner.

Comments: The rendered chicken fat adds flavor and gives the mushrooms a velvety texture. You can serve the mushrooms as is, or over a bed of stir fried vegetables such as bok choy, snow peas, Chinese broccoli, or any green vegetable. If you're using a clay pot, brown the mushrooms in a wok, then simmer in the pot.

THE PING PONG STEW

My mother was city ping pong champion during her high school years in China, much to my grandmother's dismay. Grandmother didn't feel sports were becoming to a young lady of her age. But the whole story is too long to repeat, and I've already given blow by blow coverage in my **Dim Sum** cookbook.

Today, my boys enjoy ping pong, and every so often when my mother comes to visit, they'll all play a few games together. When I made the following stew for dinner one night, one of my boys remarked, "Mom, these fish balls look just like ping pong balls."

FISHBALLS WITH BEAN CAKES AND MUSHROOMS

Yield: Serves 6 to 8

½ lb. cod, sea bass or sole, deboned and minced
½ lb. shrimp, cleaned, shelled, deveined and minced

Mix with:
  ½ cup water chestnuts, chopped
  2 green onions, chopped
  2 tsp. salt
  2 egg whites, lightly beaten
  2 tbsp. sherry
  2 tbsp. cornstarch
  ½ tsp. white pepper
8 dried Oriental mushrooms
2 medium carrots
2 pieces Chinese bean cake
4-5 iceberg lettuce leaves
2 green onions, cut into 1-inch lengths
10-12 broccoli flowerettes

Sauce mixture:
  1 cup chicken broth
  1 tbsp. Kikkoman soy sauce
  2 tbsp. sherry
  1 tbsp. oil
  1 tsp. hoisin sauce
  1 tsp. ground bean sauce
  2 tsp. hot bean sauce
  1 tsp. vinegar
  ½ tsp. sugar
2 tsp. cornstarch mixed with 1 tbsp. water

Preparation: Soak dried mushrooms for 1 hour. Squeeze dry. Reserve liquid. Discard stems and cut caps in half. Cut carrots into ⅛-inch diagonal slices. Combine sauce ingredients. Shape fish mixture into balls about the size of ping pong balls. Cut bean cake into small triangles.

Cooking: Bring 4 quarts of water to a boil and add fish balls. Quickly boil for 1 minute to give firmness. Remove with a slotted spoon. Line a clay pot or casserole dish with lettuce leaves and add fish balls, mushrooms, carrot slices and bean cake. Pour sauce over, cover and bring to a boil. Turn heat down and simmer for 15 minutes. Add the broccoli flowerettes the last 10 minutes. Stir in the cornstarch/water mixture to thicken. Add green onions. Serve.

Do-Ahead Notes: This can be made early in the day and slowly reheated.

SPICY SPARERIBS WITH BLACK BEANS

Yield: Serves 4

- 1½-2 lb. spareribs
- 2 tbsp. salted black beans
- 2 tbsp. garlic, minced
- 1 chunk fresh ginger, size of a quarter, mashed
- 3 small fresh green chili peppers, Serrano variety
- ¼ tsp. salt
- ¾ cup chicken broth
- 1 tsp. cornstarch mixed with 2 tsp. water
- 2 tbsp. oil

Preparation: Have butcher cut spareribs into 1-inch by 2-inch pieces. Wash salted black beans and mash with minced garlic. Seed chili peppers and slice into slivers.

Cooking: In a 1½-quart pot, brown spareribs in 1 tbsp. oil with the mashed ginger. Add mashed black beans, sliced green chilis and chicken broth. Cover and simmer for 20 to 30 minutes or until ⅓ cup liquid is left. Stir in the cornstarch/water mixture to thicken.

Do-Ahead Notes: Can be made 1 or 2 days in advance and reheated.

Comments: This dish is both easy and tasty. Although it's still mild, I spiced it up lightly by adding the chili peppers. Try to get the smaller ribs. They're tastier and more tender. If you're using a clay pot, brown ribs in a wok first, then transfer everything to the pot to simmer.

VEGETARIAN DELIGHT

Yield: Serves 4 to 6

- 8 dried Oriental mushrooms
- 8 fried bean cake squares, cut into halves
- 10 dried wood ears
- 3-4 cups napa cabbage, shredded
- 2-3 oz. bean threads
- 1 chunk fresh ginger, size of a quarter, mashed
- 1 medium cucumber, 5 to 6 inches long
- 1½ cups chicken broth
- 3 tbsp. dark soy sauce
- 3 tbsp. oil

Preparation: Soak wood ears and mushrooms for 1 hour. Squeeze dry. Discard mushroom stems and thinly slice caps. Nip off tough part of wood ears. Cut wood ears into small pieces. Use scissors to cut bean threads into 6-inch lengths. Pour 4 cups boiling water over bean threads and soak for ½ hour. Drain well. Seed and peel cucumber and cut into 3-inch long strips.

Cooking: In a 2½-3-quart casserole, brown mashed ginger along with all the vegetables in 3 tbsp. oil. Add bean threads and chicken broth. Cover and simmer for 15 minutes. Check to make sure there is at least ¼ cup liquid left. Add dark soy sauce.

Do-Ahead Notes: Can be made early in the day and reheated slowly.

Comments: You can buy fried bean cake squares in Chinatown, but you can do without if you can't find them. Because the bean threads and fried bean cakes absorb a great deal of liquid, we use a relatively large amount of chicken broth for simmering. The finished dish should have very little liquid left.

THE RICE CASSEROLES

The next few rice casserole recipes are truly home-style. When I was a child and very skinny, my mother made these often because she wanted me to gain weight. Knowing how much I loved these rice casseroles, she'd make them at least once or twice a week hoping I'd eat extra helpings, (and invariably I did).

These delicious and easy-to-make casseroles have the meat and seasonings cooked right into the rice so the flavors really penetrate. This is one instance where the Chinese don't eat their rice plain. For a full dinner, serve with a bowl of soup, a salad, or some stir fried vegetables.

GROUND BEEF CASSEROLE

Yield: Serves 4 to 6

    2 cups long grain rice
    1 lb. lean ground beef or ground chuck
    2 tbsp. salted turnips, minced
    3 tbsp. water chestnuts, minced
    Sauce mixture:
        2 tbsp. Kikkoman soy sauce
        2 tsp. cornstarch
        2 tbsp. water
    1 cup peas

Preparation: Wash rice 3 times, changing water each time. For the 2 cups of rice add 3 cups cold water for cooking.

Cooking: In an uncovered 3-quart pot, bring rice to a rolling boil. While you're waiting for the rice to boil, brown ground beef until done. Add minced salted turnips and water chestnuts. Add sauce mixture and stir until thickened. Push beef to one side and drain excess oil. Add the beef mixture and the peas to the rice when most of the liquid is absorbed. Cover and turn heat to the lowest point for 10 minutes. Turn off heat and wait 10 more minutes. Fluff rice and mix all

ingredients well. Serve.

Comments: Most Chinese prefer the taste of ground pork to ground beef. When beef is used, we think of this as an expensive luxury meal even though it's home-style food. Often, mothers would add more liquid to the rice and cook it a little longer so the dish would become mushy enough for baby food. It's a special treat for babies.

CHICKEN AND CHINESE SAUSAGE CASSEROLE

Yield: Serves 4 to 6

- 6 chicken thighs
- Meat marinade:
    - 2 tbsp. dark soy sauce
    - 1 tbsp. fresh ginger, minced
    - 1 tbsp. sherry
    - 1 tsp. sesame oil
- 4 Chinese sausages
- 4 dried Oriental mushrooms
- 2 cups long grain rice
- 2 green onions, minced
- 1 tbsp. light soy sauce
- 1 tsp. sesame oil

Preparation: Bone and cut chicken thighs into small cubes. Mix with meat marinade. Soak mushrooms for 1 hour, discard stems and cut caps into quarters. Add mushrooms to chicken mixture. Cut sausages into diagonal slices. Wash rice 3 times, changing the water each time. For 2 cups rice, add 3 cups cold water for cooking.

Cooking: In a 3-quart uncovered pot, bring rice to a rolling boil over high heat. Add chicken mixture and sausages to top of rice when most of the water has been absorbed. Cover pot and turn heat to lowest point for 10 minutes. Turn off heat and wait another 10 minutes. Fluff rice, mix all ingredients well and add green onions. Drizzle 1 tbsp. light soy sauce and 1 tsp. sesame oil for final flavoring.

Do-Ahead Notes: Make early in the day and reheat slowly.

Comments: It's important to use dark meat since white meat is too lean and won't stay as moist. The Chinese sausage is mild yet rich in flavor and not at all spicy. The two meats complement and enhance one another. The aroma is heavenly.

EIGHT JEWELS RICE

Yield: Serves 4 to 6

- ¾ cup long grain rice
- ¾ cup glutinous rice
- 4 dried Oriental mushrooms
- 2 Chinese sausages
- 1 set chicken giblets (liver, heart, and gizzard)
- ½ cup onion, diced
- ½ cup celery, diced
- 1 tbsp. oil
- 1-2 tbsp. light soy sauce
- ½ tsp. five spice powder
- 1 tsp. sesame oil
- ½ tsp. salt
- 2 green onions, minced

Preparation: Wash both kinds of rice together 3 times, changing the water each time. Add 2¼ cups cold water for cooking. Soak mushrooms until soft and squeeze dry. Discard stems and mince caps. Dice sausage and chicken giblets.

Cooking: Cook rice over high heat. While you're waiting for the rice to come to a boil, stir fry all ingredients except green onions in 1 tbsp. oil until done. Add light soy sauce, five spice powder, sesame oil and salt. After rice comes to a boil, add stir fried ingredients when most of the water is absorbed. Cover, turn heat to lowest point and cook for 10 minutes. Turn off heat and wait another 10 minutes. Fluff rice with minced green onions and serve.

Do-Ahead Notes: Cook early in the day and reheat in oven-proof casserole covered loosely with foil for

½ hour at 350°.

Comments: This rice is good for turkey, chicken, or game hen stuffing. An alternate method of preparing is to cook rice seperately and combine with meat mixture just after rice is done.

MORNING, NOON AND NIGHT

What food is prepared the same way for breakfast, lunch or dinner? Having a hard time thinking of one? Well, consider joak, also known as rice congee, a thick rice soup served with or without meat. It's a favorite Chinese breakfast or lunch snack and because it's both nutritious and filling, it makes an ideal family-style dinner, especially on a cold night.

JOAK (thick rice soup)

Yield: Serves 6 to 10

¾ cup long grain rice
¾ cup glutinous rice
5 qts. chicken stock
1 lb. ground pork
1 tbsp. dark soy sauce
1 tsp. salt
2 green onions
12 water chestnuts
Condiments:
  Sesame oil
  2-3 green onions, finely chopped
  White pepper
  ½ cup tea melons (sweet cucumbers), finely chopped
  1 bunch Chinese parsley, washed, patted dry and cut into ½-inch lengths
  ½ cup Szechwan pickled mustard, finely chopped
  ½ cup roasted peanuts, chopped

Preparation: Rinse rice 3 times, changing water each time. Soak overnight. Mince green onions and water chestnuts. Mix with ground pork, soy sauce and salt.

Cooking: Bring rice to a boil in chicken stock. Turn heat down and simmer for 2 to 3 hours or until it becomes thick and creamy. Turn up heat and add ground pork mixture, shaping it into small balls, one teaspoonful at a time, and dropping it into soup. Cook for 5 minutes or until pork balls are done. Correct seasoning, if necessary. Serve in individual soup bowls and pass condiments as toppings.

Do-Ahead Notes: Make early in the day and reheat slowly.

Comments: Ground beef, chicken slices or fish fillets can be substituted for pork. A roast chicken or turkey carcass is excellent for making stock. Just cook the carcass, rice and water together. Discard carcass when the soup is done.

THE BEGINNING AND THE END

When I traveled in China last year, every meal ended with a lovely bowl of soup, contrary to its first course position in the Western world. The Chinese custom really makes sense because, all too often, you get filled up too fast by drinking too much soup.

Why slave in the kitchen all day when, by the time you serve the rest of the meal, everyone already is half full from the soup? Why not serve the soup last so anyone who's still hungry can drink as much as he wants? This way, your guests will fully appreciate all the other dishes without becoming sated before they're served.

Besides, from a practical point of view, left over soup generally is easier to keep than left over stir fried dishes.

SIZZLING RICE SOUP

Yield: Serves 4 to 6

2 cups cooked rice
4 dried Oriental mushrooms, soaked and thinly sliced
¼ cup bamboo shoots, thinly sliced
¼ cup water chestnuts, thinly sliced

½ cup pork butt (about 2 oz.), thinly sliced
½ cup chicken breast (about 2 oz.), thinly sliced
Meat marinade:
   1 tsp. cornstarch
   1 tsp. Kikkoman soy sauce
   1 tsp. sherry
8 shrimp, shelled and deveined
12 snow peas
1 qt. chicken stock
2 cups oil

Preparation: Press cooked rice into a ½-inch layer in a 9-inch by 9-inch pan. Dry in a slow oven for 10 hours or longer until rice is **completely** dry and hard. Mix chicken and pork with meat marinade.

Cooking: In wok, heat 2 cups oil. Meanwhile, heat chicken stock in a 3-quart pot. When it comes to a boil, add the marinated meats, vegetables and the shrimp. Cook for 1 minute. Correct seasonings, if necessary. Ladle soup into a tureen. Deep fry rice when oil is hot. When the rice puffs up, take it out with a strainer and place in a separate bowl. Add rice to the tureen at the table. Listen to it sizzle and watch it pop!

Do-Ahead Notes: Do through preparation early in the day.

Comments: This is a delicious soup with wonderfully dramatic effects upon presentation. Because it requires last minute preparation, the rest of the dinner should consist of do-ahead dishes. Fresh water chestnuts, if they're available, are tastier then the canned variety. Make sure the oil isn't too hot or the rice will burn. The puffed rice should be lightly golden rather than deep gold or brown.

HOT AND SOUR SOUP

Yield: Serves 6 to 8

1 cup pork butt, thinly sliced
Meat marinade:
   1 tsp. Kikkoman soy sauce
   1 tsp. sesame oil
   1 tsp. cornstarch
   1 tsp. sherry
24 dried lily buds
5-6 dried Oriental mushrooms
½ cup Szechwan pickled mustard
½ cup canned bamboo shoots
1 bean cake (the firm Chinese variety)
1 qt. chicken stock
1½ tsp. salt
¼-½ tsp. white pepper, ground
2 tbsp. white vinegar
1 tbsp. dark soy sauce
2 tbsp. cornstarch mixed with 2 tbsp. water
2 eggs, beaten
½-1 tsp. hot chili oil
2 tsp. sesame oil

Preparation: Mix meat with marinade for 15 minutes. Soak lily buds with mushrooms for 1 hour. Cut off mushroom stems and slice caps, bamboo shoots, pickled mustard, and bean cakes into match stick size. Nip off tough ends of lily buds and tie a knot in the middle of each one.

Cooking: Bring stock to a boil. Add pork, lily buds, mushrooms, bamboo shoots, pickled mustard and bean cake. When stock returns to a boil, add soy sauce, white pepper, vinegar and salt. Drizzle the cornstarch/water mixture into the soup, stirring until thickened. Remove from heat, add beaten eggs and stir slowly until eggs separate into strands. Taste to see if soup is the right degree of hot and sour and adjust seasoning by adding hot chili oil if necessary. Add sesame oil just before serving. If desired, garnish with chopped green onions.

Do-Ahead Notes: This soup keeps well for several days.

...NINE DAYS OLD

If you've traveled to Hong Kong, Taiwan, or almost anywhere in the Orient, chances are you've seen the daily wash hanging by bamboo poles all over the courtyards, balconies and roof tops. Upon closer inspection, you may find a few surprises among the trousers and bed sheets. There will probably be a few ducks, fish, squid, vegetables, or just about anything edible - all food preserved by the sun. Down through the centuries this drying method was used because refrigeration was unheard of. Of course, many people now have home refrigeration, and yet the majority of the population still clings to this age-old method of food preservation. Why? Habit. Custom. But I think the real reason must be that certain foods owe their unique taste and texture to the sun drying process.

Now I'm not going to instigate a neighborhood feud by suggesting you hang out your own edible Chinese laundry. In this chapter, I'm going to show you what to do with some of these dried goodies. Perhaps you've seen these foods in Chinese groceries but had no idea what they were, much less what to do with them. I'm going to take away some of the mystery and have you cook up a few things if you're curious enough to try these recipes.

SALTED FISH

Salted fish come in varying sizes. Some are as tiny as 1-inch long while others are up to 4 pounds. They're sold by the pound so you can scoop up the little ones and experiment with a fraction of a pound. They're hard and dry and must be soaked before steaming. Most Chinese buy the larger fish whole. Keep it in the refrigerator covered with several layers of plastic wrap to prevent its odors from escaping. The most common method of cooking this fish is to cut it into small pieces, about 2-inches by 1-inch by 1-inch, and steam it with ground pork. It can also be steamed solo and served with rice.

STEAMED SMALL DRIED FISH

Yield: Serves 4

¾-1 cup tiny dried fish
4-5 slices fresh ginger
1 tsp. oil
1 tsp. Kikkoman or light soy sauce
1 tbsp. green onions, slivered

Preparation: Soak dried fish in just enough water to cover for 3 to 4 hours. Drain well. Cut sliced ginger into slivers. Mix with drained fish and place in a small, shallow, heat-proof dish.

Cooking: In wok, bring water to a boil and place the heat-proof dish on a steam rack. Cover and steam for ½ hour over medium heat. Just before serving, add oil, soy sauce, green onions and mix well.

Do-Ahead Notes: Do through preparation early in the day.

Comments: The method of eating any dried fish is to take a small amount with lots of rice. Because the fish are very salty, lots of rice is necessary to balance the taste. This has been a staple of peasants for centuries since it doesn't take much fish to feed a family. It's also nutritrious.

SALTED FISH WITH PORK PATTIES

Yield: Serves 4 to 6

    1 small chunk salted fish, about 2-inches by 1-inch by 1-inch
    1 cup ground pork (about 6 oz.)
    Meat marinade:
        1 tsp. cornstarch
        1 tsp. dark soy sauce
        ¼ tsp. sugar
    ¼ cup water chestnuts, minced
    2 tbsp. fresh ginger, slivered

Preparation: Mix pork with water chestnuts and meat marinade. Pat into a small, shallow, heat-proof dish. Wash salted fish and scrape off scales. Lightly press fish on top of the meat patty and sprinkle slivered ginger over top.

Cooking: Cover and steam over medium heat for ½ hour.

Do-Ahead Notes: Do through preparation early in the day.

Comments: My husband can be in a foul mood but everything is peachy keen again if I fix this for dinner. But I have to make sure there's plenty of rice -- four bowls is his normal capacity.

DRIED SHRIMP

    These small, dried shrimp are sold by weight with the price varying by the size of the shrimp. They're mixed with other ingredients for fillings or used as flavor enhancers in soup stock. They can also be tossed with vegetables in stir fried dishes, but in all instances, they're used sparingly. As far as I know, they're never used as the main ingredient in any dish. They aren't the stars of any meal, but they're very successful "second bananas".

DRY COOKED GREEN BEANS

Yield: Serves 4

    1½ lb. green beans
    ¼ cup pork butt (about 1 oz.), minced
    2 tbsp. dried shrimp
    1½ tbsp. Szechwan pickled mustard, minced
    1 tbsp. garlic, minced
    2 tsp. hot bean sauce
    2 cups oil

Preparation: Pinch tips of beans and string, if necessary. Don't cut them. In wok, heat oil to medium hot, about 350°. Deep fry beans, a small batch at a time, until skins begin to wrinkle and turn transparent, about 3 to 4 minutes. Remove with bamboo strainer or slotted spoon and drain on paper towel. Soak dried shrimp for 1 hour and mince.

Cooking: Heat 1 tbsp. oil. Add pork and minced shrimp and stir fry until done. Add minced pickled mustard, garlic and hot bean sauce. Stir fry for 1 minute. Add beans and keep stirring until beans are heated through. Serve.

Do-Ahead Notes: Do through preparation early in the day. The completed dish will keep well in a warm oven for 10 to 15 minutes as you go on to make other dishes. It's also good cold.

Comments: This is a popular Szechwan dish. "Dry cooked" means no liquid, such as water, is added when cooking the beans. They have a most unusual texture, a bit on the chewy side, while the dried shrimp contribute a subtle, earthy flavor. The Szechwan pickled mustard provides just enough crunch and the hot bean sauce gives it the zip so characteristic of this region's cuisine.

PRESSED DUCK

These ducks usually are hung against the wall in Chinese grocery stores. They look like they've been run over by a steam roller. Flattened like a pancake. They've been cured and dipped in oil. We like to use the bones for flavoring soups and the meat for flavoring pork and chicken in steamed dishes. Sometimes they're cooked on top of boiled rice as a flavoring agent.

STEAMED PORK WITH PRESSED DUCK

Yield: Serves 4

½-¾ lb. pork butt, thinly sliced
1 small piece pressed duck, about 1½-inches square
½ cup bamboo shoots, sliced
1 tsp. cornstarch
1 tsp. Kikkoman soy sauce
½ tsp. sugar

Preparation: Cut pressed duck into thin slices. Mix with the rest of the ingredients and press into a shallow, heat-proof dish.

Cooking: In wok, bring water to a boil. Place dish on a steaming rack, cover and steam for ½ hour over medium heat.

Do-ahead Notes: Do through preparation early in the day.

Comments: The duck has a strong flavor and is used sparingly. Now go on to the next recipe and discover how it is combined with dried vegetables to make a delicious soup.

DRIED BOK CHOY

Bok choy is grown in China and frequently is fed to the pigs. To prevent waste, it's sun dried and stored or sold in small bundles. It's said that soup made from dried bok choy soothes and clears lungs. it's also said that it supresses coughs, clears phlegm and helps sore throats.

DRIED BOK CHOY SOUP WITH PRESSED DUCK

Yield: Serves 10 to 12

    1 bundle dried bok choy
    1 pair pressed duck feet or wings or head
    6-8 jujube nuts
    4-5 Chinese dates
    2 qts. chicken stock

Preparation: Soak bok choy overnight. Clean under running water to remove sandy particles. Cut into 2-inch lengths.

Cooking: Place all ingredients in a 3 to 4-quart pot. Bring to a boil, turn heat to low, cover and simmer for 2 to 2½ hours. Correct seasoning, if necessary.

Do-Ahead Notes: Make early in the day and reheat.

Comments: This soup is on the sweet side but, oh, so good! It's truly an all-time favorite among Chinese families. What's more, I've found its medicinal claims to be absolutely true.

WET BEAN CURDS

These small bean curds are 1-inch squares resembling a cake of fresh yeast and are kept in jars on grocery shelves. They've been soaked in an alcohol-based liquid and it takes several weeks before they're ready to eat. To determine whether they're ready, turn the jar around once sharply. If the curds move *freely* in the liquid, they're ready.

Bean curds are good by themselves or can be used as a seasoning in certain stir fried dishes such as the following.

SPINACH WITH WET BEAN CURD

Yield: Serves 3 to 4

    2 bunches fresh spinach
    2 wet bean curds
    2 tbsp. oil
    2 tbsp. liquid from wet bean curd jar

Preparation: Wash spinach well. Mash bean curds with liquid from the jar.

Cooking: In wok, heat 2 tbsp. oil. Stir fry spinach until it starts to turn limp. Add bean curd mixture, tossing to mix well with spinach. Cook for 1 minute. Serve hot.

Do-Ahead Notes: Do through preparation early in the day.

Comments: Spinach cooked in this manner leaves less of a metallic after-taste.

DRIED SQUID

These are displayed in huge straw baskets along the aisles of Chinese grocery stores. They're medium brown and flattened like a pancake. We use them in stir fried dishes with vegetables.

DRIED SQUID WITH CHINESE LONG BEANS

Yield: Serves 4 to 6

    2 small dried squids
    1 bunch Chinese long beans
    1 clove garlic, mashed
    1 chunk fresh ginger, size of a quarter, mashed
    Sauce mixture:
        ⅓ cup chicken stock
        1 tsp. light soy sauce
        2 tbsp. oyster sauce
        2 tsp. cornstarch
    3 tbsp. oil
    2 tsp. baking soda

Preparation: Soak squid overnight. Clean under running water. Cut away center cartilage and other bony parts. Soak again with 2 tsp. baking soda for 15 minutes. Rinse well. Cut criss-cross scores on one side and cut into 2-inch by 1-inch pieces. Cut off tips of long beans and cut into 3-inch lengths. Wash thoroughly. Combine sauce ingredients.

Cooking: In wok, heat 1½ tbsp. oil and stir fry long beans for 1 minute. Sprinkle with salt. Add 2 tsp. water and cover for 2 to 3 minutes, or until beans are cooked but still crunchy. Set aside on serving platter. Add 1½ tbsp. oil and quickly stir fry squid, about 1 minute. They'll curl up immediately. Don't overcook. Add sauce mixture and stir until thickened. Ladle squid over beans and serve.

Do-Ahead Notes: Do through preparation.

SHRIMP PASTE

Here is the ultimate test to see if you pass for a true blue Chinese. (Ha! Ha!) I don't know the exact way of making the paste, and I really don't want to know, and neither do you. The shrimp paste comes in glass jars. One thing for certain, make sure you open it outside of the house because it has a very strong, fishy odor. It is used for seasoning certain pork and sea food dishes. The following is the most common way of using shrimp paste in a stir fried dish.

CLAMS WITH SHRIMP PASTE

Yield: Serves 4

    1½-2 lbs. small fresh clams
    ¼ lb. roast pork, thinly sliced
    ½ cup chives, cut into ½-inch lengths
    2 cloves garlic, mashed
    1 chunk fresh ginger, size of a quarter, mashed
    2-3 tbsp. shrimp paste
    2 tbsp. oil
    ½ cup chicken broth

Preparation: Soak clams 12 hours, changing water

2 or 3 times. Rinse thoroughly.

Cooking: In wok, heat oil and brown garlic and ginger. Add shrimp paste, clams, pork slices and chives. Stir fry 1 minute. Add chicken broth and simmer 3-4 minutes, or until clam shells open. Transfer to serving platter. If necessary, thicken sauce with 1 tsp. cornstarch and 1 tsp. water. Pour sauce over clams.

Do-Ahead Notes: Do through preparation.

Comments: The roast pork can be purchased in Chinatown. It's not BBQ pork. Rather, it's a roasted side of pork with a crispy skin.

LEMON PASTE (or sauce)

This is really more like a jam, and that's how I eat it on toast. It comes in glass jars, but it's easy to make at home.

LEMON PASTE

Yield: 3½ to 4 cups

10 lemons, unpeeled
2 tbsp. salt
3⅓ cups sugar

Preparation: Bring 4 to 5 quarts of water to a boil and add the whole, unpeeled lemons. When the water returns to a boil, cook the lemons 30 seconds longer. Take out with a bamboo strainer and transfer to a large glass jar. Add salt. Screw on cover. Take the jar outside and let it soak up the sun all day, every day, for 1½ to 2 months, or until lemons turn brown and soft. Quite a bit of liquid will accumulate. The length of time depends on the hotness of the climate.

To Make The Paste: Drain liquid. Mash lemons with a potato masher or in a food processor with 3⅓ cups sugar. Transfer to small jars and refrigerate another week before using. Now you have the most delicious lemon jam you've ever tasted!

Comments: The sugar is in approximate proportion, ⅓ cup per lemon, depending on their size and the degree of sweetness you prefer. It makes a welcome Christmas gift and is good on toast, muffins, or over ice cream. We also use it as a seasoning ingredient. (See Chapter 7, page 64 for a delicious and unusual **PINEAPPLE-LEMON CHICKEN** recipe.)

EGGS IN SOY SAUCE

Yield: 6 eggs

6 hard boiled eggs, peeled
1 Master Sauce recipe (page 15)

Cooking: Bring Master Sauce to a boil. Turn off heat and add eggs. When cool, refrigerate eggs in sauce for several days up to a week. Take eggs out of sauce, cut into wedges and serve as hors d'oeuvres.

Comments: The egg whites will turn a beautiful brown and absorb the Master Sauce flavor. They're tasty and unusual looking.

PICKLED VEGETABLES

Another popular way to preserve vegetables, aside from sun drying, is to pickle them in a salt and vinegar brine. The most common vegetable prepared this way is Chinese mustard greens, a leafy green vegetable with large stalks and branches. Usually, only the branches and stalks are preserved. The leaves are saved for soup. You can buy the fresh bunches and stalks for pickling in most Chinese groceries, or you can buy the vegetable already pickled. They usually are packaged in plastic. If you're unable to find Chinese mustard greens, use napa cabbage, also known as celery cabbage, or Chinese cabbage or broccoli.

PICKLED VEGETABLES

Yield: Two 1 qt. jars

2 quarts Chinese mustard greens
4 slices fresh ginger

Pickling mixture:
3 cups water
1 cup sugar
4 tsp. salt
⅔ cup cider vinegar

Preparation: Bring pickling mixture to a boil. Simmer for a few minutes until sugar and salt are dissolved. Set aside to cool thoroughly.

Break side branches off center stalk of mustard greens. Tear off leaves and save for soup. Cut branches and center stalk into 1-inch to 1½-inch chunks. Blanch them in a pot of boiling water for 1 minute. Rinse under cold water, drain, and cool thoroughly.

Clean and rinse both jars in hot water. Place mustard greens and two slices ginger root in each jar. Fill with cooled pickling mixture, cover and refrigerate for 1 week before using. Serve chilled as a side dish.

Do-Ahead Notes: Although these keep well for several months under refrigeration, they'll probably be munched up long before then.

Comments: If you're using Chinese cabbage, be sure to lightly squeeze out the liquid after parboiling it. Because Chinese cabbage contains more liquid, the pickling mixture will be diluted unless the excess is squeezed out.

THOUSAND YEAR OLD EGGS

Actually, these eggs are 100 days old, but they look like they've been around since Confucious. They're packed in a mixture of ashes, salt and lime. The egg white becomes firm and gelatinous, and its color becomes a deep amber. The yolk takes on a dark green color and its consistancy is much like a soft cheese. They require no cooking, but are cut into wedges and served as part of a cold plate, or as an accompaniment for rice congee. My favorite way to serve them is as hors d'oeuvres with thin slices of pickled ginger.

SOME LIKE IT RICH

Rich food in China doesn't mean calorie-laden sauces or cholesterol-loaded recipes since we don't use heavy cream, butter, or cheese. We also use little beef, another food associated with cholesterol. Desserts such as cakes, pies or pastries are practically nonexistent.

Rich, in the Chinese sense, means an innovative use of spices and seasoning coupled with simplicity in the cooking method to bring out the best in the food's natural taste and texture. All the recipes in this section are rich and robust in flavor, in contrast to the next chapter where the recipes are mild and delicate. Together, they complement one another in flavor, taste and texture.

SMOKING MEATS WITH SWOKE™ COOKING

Most people think of smoking meats as a long, laborious process and won't even try to find out how it's done. What if I were to tell you that you can do your own smoking right in your own kitchen in your own wok?

The folks at Taylor & Ng have devised an ingenious kit, called SWOKE™, that incorporates a wok with the ancient Chinese Smoke-Tea method. This Swoke cookery is as easy as doing a simple stir fry, or simmering a pot of soup, with equipment no more complicated than a wok and a Taylor & Ng Swoke kit. The kit consists of a Swoke rack, Swoke Cloth, Swoke Chips and Tea, and a Swoke Cooking Brochure. The metal Swoke rack fits into any 14" wok, and is similar to other steaming racks available in cookware stores. The only difference is that this rack sits much higher. This way, the meat is set far enough away from the smoking material (consisting of hickory chips or Taylor & Ng Swoke Chips, brown sugar, and tea leaves) in the bottom of the wok and won't develop black smoking lines.

Here's the basic procedure:

• Line the wok completely with heavy duty aluminum foil and place the smoking material on the bottom.

- Set the cured meat or fish on the Swoke Rack and place the wok lid over it.

- Wrap a damp towel completely around the juncture of the wok lid and Swoke Rack. The Taylor & Ng Swoke Cloth is specially designed for this purpose. Dampen the Swoke Cloth and completely cover the wok lid, rolling up the extra material in order to seal the juncture. Be sure to secure it tightly so most of the smoke won't escape.

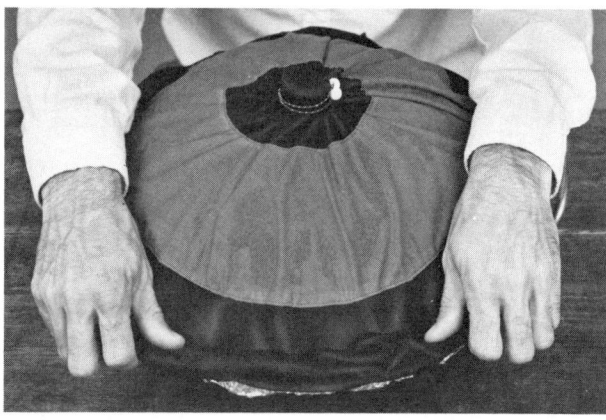

- Place the wok on medium high heat, making sure the stove's exhaust fan is turned on during the entire smoking process.

At the end of the procedure, take the wok outdoors and lift the Swoke Rack with the food on it and set aside. Wrap the smoldering smoking material in the foil and discard. Finish the rest of the cooking according to the recipe.

A chicken must be steamed before smoking, while a duck requires steaming and deep frying afterwards. The same Swoke Rack can double as a steaming rack and the same wok will hold the water needed for steaming or the oil needed for deep frying.

If you have an 1100-watt electric table top burner, so much the better. Then you can do the entire procedure -- smoking, steaming and deep frying -- outdoors. If this is the case, you don't have to wrap damp cloth around the cover since that's only a precautionary measure to keep smoke out of the kitchen. Voila! C'est tout!

SMOKE TEA DUCK

Yield: Serves 4 to 6

One 4-5 lb. duck
Curing mixture:
  4 tsp. salt
  1 tsp. Szechwan peppercorns, coarsely ground
  ¼ tsp. curing salt (saltpeter)
1 cup hickory chips or Swoke Chips
1 cup brown sugar
2 tbsp. tea leaves
Oil for deep frying

Preparation: Rub curing mixture over entire duck, inside and out. Place duck in a bowl or pan and let stand for 6 hours at room temperature. Lightly rinse off excess salt and hang duck by the neck to dry with a fan blowing on it for 6 hours, or hang overnight without a fan. The skin should be very dry at the end of the hanging period.

Smoking: Line a wok with heavy duty foil. Place a thin layer of hickory chips or Swoke Chips on the bottom, sprinkle tea leaves with brown sugar. Place duck on the Swoke Rack and cover. Dampen the Swoke Cloth and place it over the wok lid, rolling up the extra material to prevent smoke from escaping. Place wok on medium high heat and smoke for 15 minutes, starting to time after the chips begin to smoke, about 5 to 7 minutes. Don't forget to turn on the overhead fan.

Steaming: Discard the smoking material and foil. Fill bottom of wok with water to just 1-inch below the Swoke Rack. Cover again and steam duck for 1 hour. Drain liquid collected in the cavity and cool for 10 to 15 minutes.

Deep Frying: Heat 4 cups of oil in wok. Deep fry duck, ladling oil over the entire body, for 5 to 6 minutes on each side until the skin becomes crisp and turns a deep, rich reddish-brown. Cool slightly before chopping into 2-inch by 1-inch pieces.

Do-Ahead Notes: Do through steaming several hours before serving. Deep fry duck ½ hour before serving.

Comments: There are many methods of smoking duck but this is, by far, the easiest and tastiest. It's better to use a freshly dressed duck; and there's no need to wash it before rubbing it with the curing mixture. If you use a frozen duck, be sure it's completely thawed. Pat dry with paper towels so the curing mixture will be better absorbed.

Because a frozen duck usually is decapitated and there's no neck to hang it by, insert a narrow-necked bottle into the cavity and use the bottle as a base on which to stand the bird.

SMOKED FISH

Yield: Serves 4 to 6

One 2 lb. rock cod (see Comments for other fish)
Marinating mixture:
  1 tbsp. salt
  1 tbsp. fresh ginger, minced
  1 tbsp. sherry
  1 tbsp. garlic, minced
1 cup hickory chips, or Swoke Chips
1 cup brown sugar

Preparation: Score fish on each side. Rub with marinating mixture. Let stand for 4 hours at room temperature.

Smoking: Line wok with heavy duty foil. Place Swoke Chips in a thin layer on the bottom. Cover chips with brown sugar. Place fish on Swoke Rack and cover. Dampen the Swoke Cloth and place over wok lid, rolling up the extra material to prevent smoke from escaping. Smoke over medium high heat for 15 minutes, starting to time after chips begin to smoke, about 5 to 7 minutes. Don't forget to turn on your overhead fan.

Pan Frying: Add a little oil to a heated wok or skillet and pan-fry smoked fish until brown on both sides. serve hot or cold.

Do-Ahead Notes: An excellent dish to make a day ahead. If you prefer it hot, do through smoking and pan-fry at the last minute. If you plan to serve it cold, make it a day before and refrigerate.

Comments: When using a whole fish, let sit in wok an additional 20 minutes, and double marinating mixture except for salt. Add 1 tbsp. sugar. Score. This is a deliciously different way to prepare fish. It'll even delight non-fish eaters. I've also smoked salmon steaks. Slice them into ½-inch to 1-inch thick pieces, smoke for 10 minutes, then pan-fry. Fresh tuna is excellent too. Slice tuna ¼-inch thick, smoke for 6 to 7 minutes, pan-fry briefly and serve chilled as hors d'oeuvers. YUM!

SMOKED CHICKEN

Yield: Serves 4 to 6

One 4-5 lb. whole fryer
Curing mixture:
    4 tsp. salt
    1 tsp. Szechwan peppercorns, coarsely ground
    ¼ tsp. curing salt (saltpeter)
Smoking mixture:
    1 cup hickory chips, or Swoke Chips
    1 cup brown sugar

Preparation: Rub curing mixture over entire chicken, inside and out. Let stand in a bowl or pan for 6 hours. Lightly rinse off excess salt and hang chicken by the neck to dry for 6 hours with a fan blowing on it, or overnight without a fan. The skin of the chicken should be very dry.

Steaming: Fill wok with water to 1 inch below Swoke Rack. Place chicken on rack, cover and steam over medium high heat for 40-45 minutes, starting to time after water comes to a boil.

Smoking: Discard water from wok after steaming. Line wok with heavy duty aluminum foil and place 1 cup Swoke chips in a thin layer over the bottom. Add 1 cup brown sugar to cover chips. Place chicken on Swoke Rack and cover. Dampen the Swoke Cloth and place it over the wok lid, rolling up the extra material to prevent smoke from escaping. Smoke on medium heat for 15 minutes, starting to time after chips begin to smoke, about 5 to 7 minutes. Don't forget to turn on the overhead fan. Remove and cool chicken for 10 minutes. Chop into 2-inch by 1-inch pieces.

Do-Ahead Notes: Smoked chicken will keep up to ½ hour before serving. To preserve freshness and juciness, chop it just before serving.

Comments: You don't have to deep fry the chicken, as we did the duck, because the bird isn't fatty. Deep frying the duck serves to further remove the fat.

SMOKE GAME HENS L'ORANGE

Yield: Serves 6 to 8

4 game hens
Curing mixture:
    ½ tsp. curing salt (saltpeter)
    1 tbsp. salt
    Zest from 3 medium oranges
    ¾ cup Constant Comment® tea leaves
    1 cup brown sugar
    Zest from 3 oranges
Sauce mixture:
    2 tbsp. orange juice concentrate
    ½ cup plus 2 tbsp. water
    3 tbsp. sugar
    1 tsp. light soy sauce
    1 tsp. orange zest
    1 tsp. rice vinegar
    2 tsp. cornstarch

Preparation: Rub curing mixture over game hens, inside and out. Let stand in a bowl or pan for 6 hours. Insert narrow-necked bottles into the cavities and use bottles as bases for propping up hens. Dry for 6 hours with a fan blowing on them, or overnight without a fan.

Steaming: Fill wok with water to 1-inch below the Swoke Rack. Place game hens on rack, cover and bring to a boil. Lower heat to medium high and steam for 15 to 20 minutes, starting to time after water comes to a boil.

Smoking: Line wok with heavy duty foil. Place tea leaves on the bottom, cover with brown sugar and sprinkle orange zest evenly over sugar. Place game hens on Swoke Rack over the smoking material and cover. Dampen the Swoke Cloth and place it over the wok lid, rolling up the extra material to prevent smoke from escaping. Smoke on medium high heat for 15 minutes, starting to time after tea leaves begin to smoke, about 5 to 7 minutes. Don't forget to turn on the overhead fan. Remove and cool game hens for 10 minutes. To serve Chinese style, chop into 2-inch by 1-inch pieces and place sauce on the side as a dip. To serve Western style, cut birds in half and pour sauce over them.

To Make Sauce: Combine ingredients in a small pan and stir over medium heat until mixture begins to bubble and thicken.

Do-Ahead Notes: Smoked game hens keep up to ½ hour before serving. Chop just before serving to preserve freshness and juiciness. The sauce can be made earlier in the day and reheated.

Comments: You haven't lived until you've tasted this. The meat is tender, tasty and moist. They're also good the next day, and the orange flavor is even more distinct.

HOW TO KILL A CRAB

I'd like to devote a few recipes to one of my favorite shell fish -- crab. Most people who like crab won't fix it themselves. They seem to prefer the convenience of buying them already cooked. Of course, you can stir fry cooked crab, but a fresh live crab has a most delicate texture. It's definately worth that little extra time and effort to clean one yourself.

Don't kill the creature by immersing it in boiling water. If you do that, you've already cooked it. I've seen some people take the claws off, one by one, while the crab was still alive, but I can't seem to make myself do that. The quick way (for the crab) is to lay it on its backside and chop it in half. All it takes is one clean, swift stroke. The crab won't even know what happened. (Try not to chop through the back shell if you want to use it to decorate the dish.) Now, break off the claws. Open the body cavity and discard interior, especially the air sacs. Scrub the shell, legs and claws. Crack open legs and claws with the back of a cleaver. Now you're ready to proceed to the next few recipes.

GINGER CRAB WITH SHERRY

Yield: *Serves 4*
   1 large live crab, about 3 lbs.
   4 tbsp. fresh ginger, slivered
   3 tbsp. garlic, minced
   2 tsp. salt
   3-4 tbsp. sherry
   4 green onions, cut into 1-inch lengths
   3-4 tbsp. oil

Preparation: Prepare crab according to directions on this page.

Cooking: Heat wok until hot. Add oil and ginger. When oil is hot, add garlic and crab pieces. Stir fry over high heat until crab turns red. Add salt, sherry and green onions and stir fry for 3 to 4 minutes. If sherry evaporates too quickly, drizzle more along the side of the wok. Correct seasoning, if necessary, and serve.

CRAB IN PEKING SAUCE

Yield: *Serves 4*
   1 large live crab, about 3 lbs.
   3 tbsp. fresh ginger, minced
   3 tbsp. garlic, minced
   4 green onions, cut into 1-inch pieces
  Sauce mixture:
     2 tbsp. hoisin sauce
     2 tbsp. sweet bean sauce
     ½ cup chicken broth
   3-4 tbsp. oil

Preparation: Prepare crab according to directions on this page. Combine sauce ingredients.

Cooking: Heat wok until hot. Add oil and ginger. When oil is hot, add garlic and crab pieces. Stir fry over high heat until crab turns red. Add sauce and green onions. Cook for 2 to 3 minutes more, stirring and basting crab with sauce. Serve.

Comments: Once you've tasted fresh crab prepared this way, you'll never want to use cooked crab again. If you use the back shell for decoration, dunk it in a pot of hot water until it turns red. Then, after you've finished stir frying the crab pieces, add the shell for a last minute mixing with the sauce. Arrange crab pieces around shell.

CURRIED CRAB

Yield: *Serves 4*

    1 large live crab, about 3 lbs.
    2 tbsp. fresh ginger, minced
    2 tbsp. garlic, minced
    4 green onions, cut into 1-inch lengths
    Sauce mixture:
        2 tbsp. curry powder
        1 tsp. salt
        1 tsp. light soy sauce
        1 tbsp. oyster sauce
        ½ cup chicken broth
        ½ tsp. sugar
        2 tsp. cornstarch mixed with 1 tbsp. water
    3-4 tbsp. oil

Preparation: Prepare crab according to directions on page 43. Combine sauce ingredients.

Cooking: Heat wok until hot. Add oil and ginger. When oil is hot, add garlic and crab pieces. Stir fry over high heat until crab turns red. Add sauce and green onions. Cook for 2 to 3 minutes more, stirring, and basting crab pieces with the sauce. Add cornstarch mixture to thicken and serve.

CRAB IN BLACK BEAN SAUCE

Yield: *Serves 4*

    1 large live crab, about 3 lbs.
    3 tbsp. fresh ginger, minced
    3 tbsp. garlic, minced
    2 tbsp. salted black beans, rinsed
    Sauce mixture:
        ½ cup chicken broth
        1 tbsp. Kikkoman soy sauce
        ½ tsp. sugar
        1 tsp. sesame oil
        2 tsp. cornstarch mixed with 1 tbsp. water
    3 green onions, cut into 1-inch lengths
    3-4 tbsp. oil

Preparation: Prepare crab according to directions on page 43. Combine sauce ingredients. Mash black beans, ginger and garlic together.

Cooking: Heat wok until hot. Add oil and black bean mixture. When the flavor is released, about 15 seconds, add crab pieces and stir fry over high heat until crab turns red. Add sauce and green onions. Cook for 2 to 3 minutes more, stirring and basting crab pieces with sauce. Add cornstarch mixture to thicken and serve.

STUFFED PHOENIX TAIL PRAWNS

Yield: *Serves 4*

    16 large prawns
    Stuffing mixture:
        ½ cup fresh pork sausage
        2 dried Oriental mushrooms
        4 water chestnuts, minced
        1 green onion, minced
        ¼ tsp. sugar
        ⅛ tsp. white pepper
        1 tsp. sherry
    2 eggs, beaten
    Flour mixture:
        ½ cup flour
        ½ cup cornstarch
        1 tsp. salt
    Sauce mixture:
        ½ cup chicken broth
        1 tsp. sugar
        1 tsp. Kikkoman soy sauce
        1 tsp. sesame oil
        1½ tsp. white vinegar
        1 tsp. sweet bean sauce
        1 tsp. hoisin sauce
    2 green onions, chopped
    3 cups oil

Preparation: Shell, devein and clean prawns leaving tails intact. To butterfly prawns, cut lengthwise along underside. Don't cut completely through. Lay prawn on a cutting board and flatten with a cleaver. Now make an outward lateral cut with the cleaver blade on each side of the thickest part of the prawn (the upper third section).

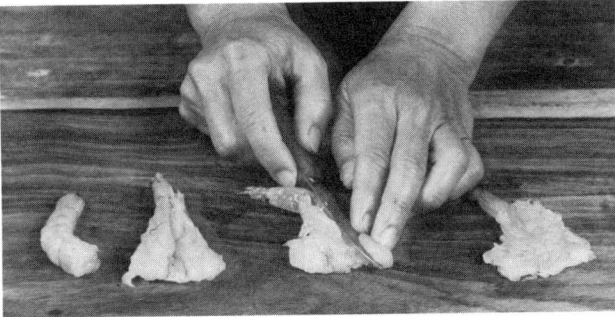

Lay open again and flatten with cleaver. Soak dried mushrooms for 1 hour. Discard stems and mince caps. Combine ingredients for stuffing and sauce. Spread a thin layer of stuffing on an opened prawn and press another prawn on top.

Dip prawns into the beaten egg, then dip into the flour mixture. Repeat the dipping process one more time.

Cooking: In wok, heat 3 cups of oil. Deep fry prawns until golden. Drain on paper towel. Transfer to serving platter and arrange in sunburst fashion. Cook sauce until thickened and pour over prawns. Garnish with green onions.

Do-Ahead Notes: Deep fry prawns several hours in advance. Deep fry again just before serving.

Comments: Don't make the stuffing layer too thick, as it would require too much time to cook the sausage, and the prawns would be overcooked.

SUB GUM FISH

Yield: Serves 4 to 6

One 2-2½ lb. rock cod
½ cup carrots, slivered
½ cup green onions, slivered
½ cup dried Oriental mushrooms, soaked for 1 hour
2-3 tbsp. fresh ginger, slivered
½ cup pork butt (about 2 oz.), cut into thin strips
Meat marinade:
 1 tsp. cornstarch
 1 tsp. Kikkoman soy sauce
 1 tsp. sherry
2 tbsp. garlic, minced
Sauce mixture:
 ⅓ cup water from soaked mushrooms
 ⅓ cup chicken broth
 2 tsp. light soy sauce
 1½ tsp. sugar
 1½ tsp. sesame oil
 1 tbsp. oyster sauce
 2½ tsp. cornstarch
 2 tbsp. sherry
 1 tsp. rice vinegar
3-4 cups oil for deep frying

Preparation: Make 4 deep, slanted cuts on each side of fish. Sprinkle with salt and dredge in cornstarch. Squeeze soaked mushrooms dry, discard stems and cut caps into thin slices. Mix pork slices with meat marinade. Combine sauce ingredients.

Cooking: In wok, heat 3 to 4 cups oil. When oil is hot, deep fry fish about 6 minutes on one side. Turn fish over and fry another 3 to 4 minutes. It's done when a chopstick can be inserted through the thickest part without resistance. While fish is deep frying, in another wok or skillet, stir fry pork slices with minced garlic, carrots, mushrooms and ginger. Add green onions and sauce when pork appears done, about 1 to 2 minutes. Stir until thickened. Keep warm. Remove fish, drain, place on serving platter and pour sauce over it.

Do-Ahead Notes: Deep fry fish several hours in advance. Cook meat with sauce mixture. Don't add green onions until just before serving to insure freshness. Just before serving, deep fry fish briefly once again to crisp texture.

Comments: You'll receive rave notices every time you serve this delicious fish. The required deep frying time depends on the thickness of the fish, so use your common sense and don't overcook.

STUFFED BEAN CAKES

Yield: Serves 4

    2 Chinese bean cakes
    Stuffing:
        4 shrimp, minced
        2 oz. cod, bass, or sole fillet, minced
        2-4 water chestnuts, minced
        1 green onion, minced
        ½ tsp. sherry
        ¼ tsp. salt
        1 small egg white
        A few dashes white pepper
    24 snow peas, washed and strung
    6 dried Oriental mushrooms, soaked 1 hour
    1 small carrot, cut to match stick size
    Sauce mixture:
        1 tsp. light soy sauce
        1 tsp. hoisin sauce
        1 tsp. ground bean sauce
        2 tbsp. oyster sauce
        1 tsp. rice vinegar
        2 tsp. cornstarch
    1 cup chicken broth

2 green onions, cut into 1-inch strips
2-3 cups oil

Preparation: Press bean cakes for 6 to 8 hours by placing a wooden board over them and topping it with a heavy book or water-filled pot. Drain off liquid occasionally.

Cut each bean cake into 4 triangles and make a deep slit in each triangle to form a pocket. Fill with stuffing.

Cut each triangle in half.

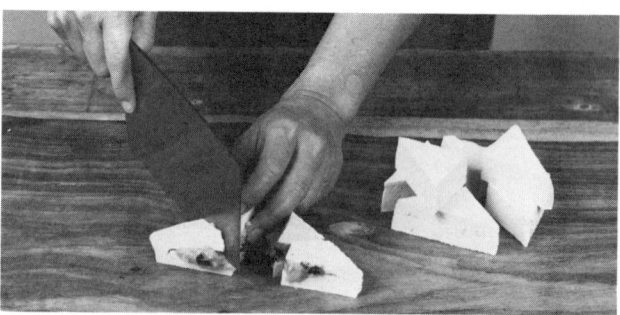

Deep fry in hot oil until bean cake is golden, about 3 to 4 minutes. Drain. Cut stems off mushrooms, discard, and cut caps into thin slices. Combine sauce ingredients.

Cooking: In wok, heat 1 tbsp. oil and stir fry all the vegetables except green onions for 1 to 2 minutes. Set aside. Add deep fried bean cakes and chicken broth. Cook over medium heat until bean cakes are heated through, about 1 to 2 minutes. Add sauce mixture and cook until thickened. Add vegetables and green onions. Mix well and serve.

Do-Ahead Notes: Do through preparation early in the day.

Comments: Bean cakes contain a lot of water and must be pressed so they'll deep fry properly. Otherwise, with so much water in the hot oil, you'll have oil popping all over the kitchen. By cooking the deep fried bean cakes in the chicken broth, moisture is returned and flavor added. Red bell pepper can be substituted for carrot. You may use a food processor to make the filling.

FAMILY STYLE BEAN CAKES

Yield: Serves 4

> 4 Chinese bean cakes
> ¼ lb. snow peas
> 10-12 dried Oriental mushrooms.
> Sauce mixture:
> > 3 tbsp. Kikkoman soy sauce
> > 1 tsp. sugar
> > ½ tsp. salt
> > ¾ cup chicken stock
> > 1 tbsp. garlic, minced
> > ½ cup green onions, coarsely chopped
> > 1 tbsp. cornstarch mixed with 2 tbsp. water
> > 1 cup oil

Preparation: Press bean cakes for ½ hour to eliminate excess liquid. (See previous recipe for method). Cut each cake in the following manner: Slice once through cross section to produce two thin slabs.

Quarter each cross section so each piece will yield four 1-inch by 2-inch by ½-inch pieces. Wash and string snow peas. Soak mushrooms ½ hour, discard stems and cut caps in half. Combine sauce ingredients.

Cooking: In wok, heat 1 cup oil until hot. Fry bean cakes 5 or 6 pieces at a time, turning each slice until golden on both sides. Set aside. Drain off all but 2 tbsp. oil. Stir fry mushrooms with snow peas for 1 minute. Add bean cakes, green onions, and sauce and continue cooking for 1 to 2 minutes. Toss gently to make sure bean cakes are well coated with sauce. Thicken with cornstarch/water mixture and serve.

Do-Ahead Notes: Bean cakes may be fried early in the day.

Comments: This is an excellent vegetarian dish. You can add ½ cup sliced pork, but I find the dish good without meat. The bean cake absorbs the flavor of the sauce and becomes very tasty. You can use the water from the soaked mushrooms as part of the chicken stock.

ABALONE AND MUSHROOMS IN OYSTER SAUCE

Yield: Serves 4 to 6

> ⅓-½ lb. fresh abalone
> 12 medium dried Oriental mushrooms
> ¼ tsp. salt
> ¼ tsp. sugar
> 1 chunk fresh ginger, size of a half dollar, crushed
> Sauce mixture:
> > 2 tsp. cornstarch
> > ½ cup chicken broth
> > 2 tsp. sherry
> > 2 tbsp. oyster sauce
> > 1 tbsp. light soy sauce
> > 1 tsp. sugar
> 3 tbsp. oil
> 2 green onions, cut into 1-inch lengths

Preparation: Slice abalone as thin as possible, then pound each slice with meat mallet to break down the fiber. Soak mushrooms for 1 hour. Discard stems. Combine sauce ingredients.

Cooking: Heat 3 tbsp. oil in wok. Brown ginger,

abalone, mushrooms, salt and sugar for 1 to 1½ minutes. Add sauce mixture and stir until thickened. Add green onions, mix well and serve.

Do-Ahead Notes: Do through preparation several hours in advance.

Comments: Abalone will get tough if overcooked, so be cautious. Canned abalone also can be used, in which case it needs no pounding.

BEEF ON A STICK

Yield: 24 to 30 sticks

1-1⅓ lb. flank steak
Meat marinade:
⅓ cup Kikkoman soy sauce
⅓ cup sugar
1½ tbsp. hoisin sauce
2 tbsp. cornstarch
1 tbsp. garlic, minced
1 tbsp. fresh ginger, minced
3-4 cups oil
24-30 bamboo skewers

Preparation: Slice flank steaks cross-grain about ⅛-inch thick. Mix meat marinade and pour over meat. Mix well to be sure each strip is covered. Refrigerate 24 hours or overnight. Skewer each strip of meat with bamboo skewer.

Cooking: Heat oil in wok until hot. Deep fry meat sticks, several at a time for 20 seconds, turning over once after the first 10 to 12 seconds. Drain on platter and serve hot.

Do-Ahead Notes: Do through preparation.

Comments: I first tasted this delicious concoction in a small Southern California Chinese restaurant. It's similar to Japanese Beef Teriyaki, but this version has a beautiful glaze and, of course, it has that unique Chinese flavor. it was so good I was determined to duplicate the recipe even if I had to make a special trip down there to sample it again. Fortunately, another business trip required me to return, and I immediately showed up at the restaurant to order more of their delicious beef sticks. This time, I ate slowly and tried to analyse the flavor and cooking method. I was truly surprised when I managed to duplicate its taste and texture successfully at the first try.

ROAST DUCK IN HOISIN SAUCE

Yield: Serves 4 to 6

One 4-5 lb. duck
1 tbsp. salt
1 tsp. five spice powder
Sauce mixture:
1½ tbsp. ground bean sauce
1½ tbsp. hoisin sauce
2 tbsp. catsup
1 tbsp. dark soy sauce
1 tbsp. brown sugar
¼ cup dark soy sauce
¼ cup maple syrup

Preparation: Pierce skin of duck with fork. Cut off tail. Fill a deep pot with enough water to cover duck. Bring water to a boil and immerse duck for 2 minutes. Lift duck out, drain and pat dry. Rub cavity and the entire body with five spice powder, salt, and then the sauce mixture. Let stand for 8 hours.

Cooking: Preheat oven to 400°. Line roasting pan

with foil and pour ½ to 1 cup water into pan. Rub dark soy sauce and maple syrup over the entire duck and place it on the roasting rack, back side up. Roast for ½ hour or until golden brown. Turn the duck breast side up and lower temperature to 325°. Roast 40 minutes more. Brush on extra soy sauce and maple syrup during roasting. The duck should be nice and brown. Take out and cool for 10 to 15 minutes. Chop into 2-inch by 1-inch pieces. Serve as is or with plum sauce as a dip.

Do-Ahead Notes: Do through preparation.

Comments: The water in the roasting pan will catch the fat from the duck and prevent it from smoking in the oven. Because it's been marinated a long time, the duck meat will be extremely tasty.

CHICKEN WINGS WITH MUSHROOMS

Yield: Serves 6 to 8
20 chicken wings

Cooking sauce mixture:
1½ cups dark soy sauce
½ cup light soy sauce
2 cups water
8 tbsp. vinegar
1 star anise
1 chunk fresh ginger, size of a quarter, crushed
5-6 cloves garlic, mashed
12 medium fresh mushrooms
1 tbsp. oil
½ tsp. salt
2 tbsp. sherry
Thickening sauce mixture:
1½ cups cooking sauce after wings have been cooked in it
2 tbsp. cornstarch
2 tbsp. oyster sauce
2 green onions, chopped

Preparation: Cut tips off wings and save for making stock. Cut each wing again at the joint. Wash mushrooms and cut in half.

Cooking: Bring cooking sauce mixture to a boil and add chicken wings. Bring sauce back to a boil, cover and lower heat to simmer. Cook for 10 minutes. Turn off heat. Stir wings so all are evenly colored by the sauce. Let stand for ½ hour.

Heat 1 tbsp. oil in wok and stir fry mushrooms for a few seconds. Add salt and sherry and continue stirring for 1 minute. Add thickening sauce and stir until thickened. Add wings. Mix well. Garnish with green onions.

Do-Ahead Notes: Make several hours in advance and reheat in wok.

Comments: This is a good dish to prepare for a crowd. Serve it with a salad and rice. The sauce is especially good over plain boiled rice.

BANQUET PORK

Yield: Serves 4 to 6

1 lb. pork butt
1 Master Sauce recipe (see page 15)
1 bunch fresh spinach
Sauce for topping:
¼ cup Master Sauce
¼ cup water
2 tsp. sherry
¼ tsp. sesame oil
½ tsp. sugar
5 dashes white pepper
1 tbsp. cornstarch

Preparation: Slice pork butt no more than 1-inch thick. Simmer Master Sauce. Wash spinach, then blanch in water for 30 seconds, drain and dry well. Mix sauce topping ingredients.

Cooking: Cook pork in simmering Master Sauce for 40 minutes. Remove and cool on platter. Cut into thin slices (A). Cook topping sauce until thickened.

Assembling: Place spinach on round serving platter. Arrange pork in layers in round soup bowl, ladling a small amount of topping sauce between every other layer (B and C) of pork ending with sauce on the top layer. Reserve 2 tbsp. sauce. Place bowl on steaming rack, cover and steam until heated through - about 20 minutes. Invert on top of spinach, add remaining 2 tbsp. of topping sauce (D) and decorate with fresh Chinese parsley sprigs.

Do-Ahead Notes: Do through assembling layers of pork several hours in advance. Steam just before serving.

Comments: Instead of blanching, spinach can be stir-fried 1-2 minutes in 1 tbsp. oil with ½ tsp. salt for a better flavor.

SOME LIKE IT MILD

The most unique feature of a Chinese dinner is the enjoyment of a wide spectrum of different tastes in one meal. Sweet and sour. Hot and spicy. Bland and mild. Rich and robust. Even bitter as in bitter melons. Think how dull a meal would be if all the food were of one flavor. All hot, or all sour. All sweet, or all spicy. After a few bites, I'm sure you'd lose interest, and your taste buds would call it a night.

On the other hand, if you're able to savor the sweet against the sour, the spicy against the bland, or the hot against the cool; you enjoy the meal with a great deal more enthusiasm. Each flavor enhances the other and you discover new sensations and tastes with each bite.

This chapter provides such a contrast. These dishes are mild compared to recipes from other chapters. Some are downright bland. They offer the necessary balance to a hearty dish or a hot and spicy concoction.

DICED PORK IN LETTUCE CUPS

Yield: Serves 8 to 10

    1 cup pork butt (about 8 oz.), finely diced
    Meat marinade:
        1 tsp. cornstarch
        1 tsp. dark soy sauce
        ½ tsp. sherry
        ½ tsp. sesame oil
    ½ cup frozen peas
    ½ cup water chestnuts, diced
    ½ cup bamboo shoots, diced
    ½ cup Chinese sausage, diced
    ½ cup onion, diced
    ½ cup canned mushrooms (stems and pieces)
    ½ cup green onions, diced
    Sauce mixture:
        ⅓ cup chicken broth
        1 tsp. light soy sauce
        1 tsp. dark soy sauce
        1 tsp. sesame oil
        1 tsp. sherry
        2 tbsp. oyster sauce
        2 tsp. cornstarch
    2 tbsp. oil
    1 head iceberg lettuce

Preparation: Mix meat with marinade. Combine sauce ingredients. wash lettuce, separate each leaf, dry well and keep chilled.

Cooking: Heat wok and add 1 tbsp. oil. Stir fry all vegetables plus the sausage. Set aside. Add 1 tbsp. oil and stir fry diced pork. Add sauce mixture and vegetables. Stir until thickened. Spoon mixture into lettuce leaves, wrap securely and eat while hot.

Do-Ahead Notes: Do through preparation several hours in advance. The stir fried mixture will keep in a 200° oven for 10 to 15 minutes.

Comments: This is a famous Cantonese banquet dish. Usually, the meat is either squab or dried oysters. Since these are rather difficult to find in this country, and are very expensive, I've substituted pork. If you omit the meat, it becomes a delightful vegetarian dish. The feeling of biting into a hot filling surrounded by chilled lettuce is sensational!

VELVETING

Velveting is a special cooking procedure found mainly in Northern, Szechwan and Hunan cuisine. There are two methods of velveting -- one in oil, the other in water. The former method is practiced widely in expensive restaurants and wealthy homes because it requires a lot of oil. The poor peasants simply can't afford that kind of luxury, so they use water instead.

Any kind of meat or seafood can be velveted. The procedure is simple. The meat generally is marinated in egg whites, cornstarch, salt and sherry first. Then it's cooked in 2 to 3 cups of oil heated to just above the warm stage. (If you drop a piece of green onion in it, it'll **barely** sizzle). The meat is stirred with chopsticks to separate the pieces and insure even cooking. It's taken out as soon as it is **just** done. The texture of the meat is velvety smooth.

The meat should be sliced as thin as possible to insure even cooking in the shortest possible time. The egg white coating adds to the smooth texture and, often, the meat is lightly pounded with a cleaver to further break down the meat fiber.

The oil must be at the proper temperature. Hot oil will cause the meat to brown too quickly and stick to the bottom of the wok. Even worse, the texture will be tough and dry, especially in the case of chicken.

Even the act of stirring has great consequence. You must stir in one direction only since centrifugal force causes the egg white to adhere to the meat. If you stir every which way, the egg white will separate.

After the meat is properly velveted, it can be combined with other vegetables and sauces without further cooking.

The procedure for water velveting is exactly the same as for oil velveting. It's more economical, and I'm sure people on a restricted diet will welcome the idea.

Several velveting recipes follow. Don't be discouraged if the meat doesn't turn out velvety smooth the first time. Mine didn't. It takes practice, but when you do it right, there's no other texture quite like it. C'est magnifique!

VELVET CHICKEN WITH SPINACH

Yield: Serves 3 to 4

    1 whole chicken breast
    Meat marinade:
        1 tbsp. cornstarch
        1 tsp. sherry
        2 egg whites, lightly beaten
        1½ tsp. oil
        ¾ tsp. salt
    1 bunch fresh spinach, washed and drained

Preparation: Bone and skin chicken breast. Pound breast first with the flat side of a meat cleaver, then with the back side, then again with the flat side. Partially freeze for 1 to 2 hours. Slice as thin as possible. Mix with meat marinade for 15 minutes. Blanch spinach in boiling water for 30 seconds and drain.

Cooking: Heat 2 cups of oil in wok until it is just past the warm stage. Add half of the chicken (it will just barely sizzle) and stir with chopsticks until it just turns white. Take out quickly with a bamboo strainer and cook the next batch. Place spinach on a platter, then top with chicken.

Do-Ahead Notes: Do through preparation

Comments: You may prefer to quickly stir fry the spinach instead of blanching it, since it's more flavorful that way. However, blanching will save you some last minute work.

This is a simple, yet elegant dish in which the texture of the chicken is all important. Be sure to read the section on velveting before you try this, or any other velveting recipes.

The amount of egg whites depends on the size of the chicken breast as well as the size of the eggs.

Make sure each slice of chicken is coated with the egg white mixture. The marinated meat should feel slippery, not sticky. If it's sticky, add another lightly beaten egg white.

BEEF WITH CHIVES

Yield: Serves 4 to 6

¾ lb. flank steak
Meat marinade:
    2 egg whites, lightly beaten
    1 tbsp. cornstarch
    ½ tsp. salt
Sauce mixture:
    3 tbsp. Kikkoman soy sauce
    1 tbsp. dark soy sauce
    1½ tbsp. brown sugar
    1 tbsp. sesame oil
    2 tsp. rice vinegar
    1 tbsp. sherry
    1 tbsp. garlic, minced
1 tsp. cornstarch mixed with 2 tsp. water
1 small bunch chives, cut into 2-inch lengths
2 cups oil

Preparation: Cut flank steak cross-grain into ⅛-inch slices. Mix with meat marinade. Combine sauce ingredients..

Cooking: In wok, heat 2 cups oil until medium hot, about 250° to 275°. Deep fry beef slices in 3 batches until just done, less than 1 minute. Drain off all but 2 tbsp. oil. Pour in sauce mixture and reduce 1½ to 2 minutes over high heat. Add chives, then beef slices and stir until well mixed. If the sauce appears thin, add some of the cornstarch/water mixture to thicken slightly.

Do-Ahead Notes: Do through preparation early in the day.

Comments: If you can't find chives, substitute leeks or green onions. I've tried all three and all are wonderful and unique. In China, yellow chives are preferred to green chives because the color gives the dish a bright and unusual appearance, although the taste is the same.

TREASURE CHICKEN

Yield: Serves 4 to 6

1 whole chicken breast
Meat marinade:
    1 tbsp. cornstarch
    1 tsp. sherry
    2 egg whites, lightly beaten
    1½ tsp. oil
    ½ tsp. salt
¼ lb. snow peas
1 small red bell pepper (or 1 carrot)
6 water chestnuts (or equal amount of jimaca)
Sauce mixture:
    ½ cup chicken broth
    2 tsp. cornstarch
1 tbsp. rendered chicken fat
2 cups oil

Preparation: Bone and skin chicken breast. Pound breast first with the flat side of a meat cleaver, then the back side, then the flat side again. Partially freeze for 1-2 hours. Slice thin. Mix with meat marinade for ½ hour. Wash and string snow peas. Cut red bell pepper into small, diagonal slices. Peel and thinly slice water chestnuts. Mix sauce ingredients.

Cooking: Heat 2 cups oil in wok until just past the warm stage. Add ½ of the chicken (it will barely sizzle) and stir with chopsticks until it just turns white. Take out quickly with a bamboo strainer and repeat with the next batch. Pour off all but 2 tbsp. oil. Stir fry vegetables for 2 minutes, sprinkle lightly with salt to taste and add ¼ tsp. sugar. Pour in sauce mixture and stir until thickened. Add rendered chicken fat and chicken breast. Mix quickly and serve.

Do-Ahead Notes: Do through preparation early in the day.

Comments: Green snow peas represent jade, red bell pepper is ruby, and white water chestnuts are pearls. Hence the name, Treasure Chicken. Rendered chicken fat is added at the last minute for flavor. The amount of egg white depends on the size of the chicken breast and the size of the egg. After mixing with the marinade, the chicken slices should feel slippery.

Fresh water chestnuts are incomparable in taste and texture. Fresh jimaca, found in the produce section of many grocery stores, is a good substitute. Use canned water chestnuts only as a last resort.

CHICKEN IN GARLIC AND GINGER SAUCE

Yield: Serves 4

    One 2½ lb. whole fryer
    1 tbsp. rendered chicken fat
    2 cloves garlic, minced
    2 tbsp. fresh ginger, slivered
    ¾ cup chicken broth
    ¼ tsp. sugar
    ¼ tsp. salt
    1 tbsp. cornstarch mixed with 2 tbsp. water
    2 green onions, slivered into 1-inch lengths

Preparation: Bring 4 quarts of water to a boil with 2 tbsp. salt. Immerse cleaned chicken in the boiling water and wait for it to return to a boil. Cover and turn off heat immediately. Let steep for 30 minutes. Lift chicken out and rinse under cold water for 2 to 3 minutes. Let it cool.

Cooking: Heat rendered fat with garlic and ginger in a small sauce pan. Add chicken broth, sugar and salt. Simmer for 2 to 3 minutes. Add cornstarch/water mixture. Stir until thickened. Add green onions just before serving.

Assembling: Chop chicken into 2-inch by 1-inch pieces. Arrange attractively on platter. Pour hot sauce over chicken and serve.

Do-Ahead Notes: Sauce can be made in advance and chicken can be cooked 1 hour before serving. Chop chicken ½ hour before serving and keep moist with plastic wrap.

Comments: This is a most delicious recipe because you can truly taste the chicken flavor. When cooked by the steeping method, the bird stays juicy and tender. A fresh dressed chicken from a Chinatown is much better than those found in the supermarket, beacuse its skin has a firmer and crispier texture. That's the reason for rinsing it under cold water after it's cooked -- to better bring out the texture of the skin as well as to stop it from cooking further. The bird should be barely done and the bone marrow of its thigh should be bright red. That's the way we consider a chicken properly cooked. We don't like the meat to fall off the bone. That's not cooking. That's cremation.

FRAGRANT CRISPY CHICKEN

Yield: Serves 4

    One 2-2½ lb. whole fryer
    Seasoning mixture:
        ½ tsp. five spice powder
        1½ tsp. salt
        ½ tsp. Szechwan peppercorns, finely ground
    Basting mixture:
        1 tbsp. dark soy sauce
        1 tbsp. maple syrup
        1 tbsp. cornstarch
        1 tbsp. vinegar
        ¼ cup water
    ½-¾ cup cornstarch
    4-5 cups oil

Preparation: Rub fryer with seasoning mixture. Place chicken on a heat-proof plate and set on a steaming rack. Cover. Bring water to a boil and turn heat down so water is barely simmering. Steam chicken for ½ hour. Remove chicken and let cool for 15 minutes. While cooling, baste chicken with basting mixture several times, holding chicken over a large bowl to catch the drippings. Pat a thick coat of cornstarch over entire chicken and hang up to dry for 8 hours or overnight. The skin should be very dry to insure crispness when deep fried.

Cooking: Heat oil in wok until hot. Deep fry chicken until nicely browned on both sides. Spoon hot oil over chicken as it's frying to insure even coloring. Lift out and drain oil. Let cool for a few minutes before chopping into 1-inch by 2-inch pieces. Arrange on a bed of lettuce.

Do-Ahead Notes: Do through preparation.

Comments: Don't use a chicken any larger than specified, or the wok won't be able to accomodate it. When properly prepared, the skin is light and crispy, and the meat is tender and juicy.

FISH FILLET IN BLACK BEAN SAUCE

Yield: Serves 4

¾ lb. rock cod fillet
Fish marinade:
  2 egg whites
  1 tsp. sherry
  ½ tsp. salt
  1 tbsp. cornstarch
2 tbsp. salted black beans, washed
1 tbsp. garlic, minced
1 tbsp. fresh ginger, minced
1 green pepper, cut into 1-inch cubes
1 small onion, cut into wedges
Sauce mixture:
  ½ cup chicken stock
  1 tsp. cornstarch

Preparation: Cut fish into 1½-inch pieces. Mix with marinade and let stand ½ hour. Mash black beans, minced ginger and minced garlic with 1 tsp. water. Combine sauce ingredients.

Cooking: Bring 4 quarts water with 1 tbsp. of oil to a boil. Turn heat down and wait until water returns to a bare simmer. Gently drop fish pieces into the hot water and simmer for 1 minute or just until done. Remove with bamboo strainer. Meanwhile, heat wok, add 1 tbsp. oil and stir fry pepper and onion with black bean sauce. Add sauce mixture and stir until thickened. Add cooked fish fillets and toss gently to mix.

Do-Ahead Notes: Do through preparation early in the day.

Comments: Fish fillet is delicate and velveting will bring out that fragile texture in addition to keeping each piece whole. Stir frying may have a tendency to break up the pieces because of the constant turning. Try sea bass, red snapper or perch as equally delicious substitutes.

SCALLOPS WITH SNOW PEAS

Yield: Serves 4

¾ lb. scallops
¼ lb. snow peas
8 Oriental dried mushrooms, soaked for 1 hour
½ cup carrots, thinly sliced diagonally
Sauce mixture:
  ¼ cup chicken broth
  1 tsp. cornstarch
1 tbsp. garlic, minced
1 tbsp. fresh ginger, minced
2 green onions, cut into 1-inch lengths
3 tbsp. oil

Preparation: Drain and squeeze all liquid from scallops. Cut cross-grain into ¼-inch slices. Wash and string snow peas. Discard mushroom stems and cut caps in half. Parboil carrots for 1 minute. Drain. Combine sauce ingredients.

Cooking: Heat wok until hot. Add 1 tbsp. oil and stir fry snow peas, mushrooms and carrots about 1½ to 2 minutes. Add 1 tsp. sherry and season with a little salt and sugar. Cook 1 to 2 minutes and set aside. Heat 2 tbsp. oil with ginger. Add garlic and scallops. Stir fry about 1½ minutes. Add cornstarch mixture. When thickened, add green onions and vegetables. Mix well and serve.

Do-Ahead Notes: Do through preparation several hours in advance.

Comments: Scallops must be squeezed dry, or they'll get too watery when cooked. The wok must be very hot so it will sear the scallops the minute they hit. Don't overcook, or the texture will be coarse and chewy. Since scallops have a delicate taste and texture, only a light sauce is used to enhance them.

POT STICKERS

Yield: 4 doz.

Dough:
4 cups sifted all-purpose flour
1 cup plus 2 tbsp. warm water

To Make Dough: Mix flour with warm water and knead for 10 minutes. There is no need to add any flour on the board as you knead because the dough should be at a perfect consistency. Let dough rest for 20 minutes while you make the filling.

Filling:
1 lb. fresh ground pork
1½ to 2 cups shredded napa cabbage
1 tbsp. light soy sauce
1 tbsp. sherry
1 tbsp. sesame oil
1¼ tsp. salt
3 tbsp. minced green onions
3 tbsp. minced fresh ginger
3 tbsp. minced Chinese parsley (cilentro)

To Make Filling: Mix all ingredients and chill for 4 hours or overnight before wrapping.

Wrapping: Divide dough into 4 parts. Roll each part out to about 12 inches in length and divide into 12 balls. Roll each ball into 3-inch round flat discs and drop 1 tbsp. of filling in the center. Fold the dough over the filling, pinching together just the top to make a half circle. On the side nearest you, form 2 pleats on each side and pinch them to meet the opposite side to seal.

Cooking: Place 2 tbsp. oil in a 12-inch skillet with a non-stick finish. Arrange potstickers in the skillet and add enough water to cover half of the potstickers. Cover and bring the water to a boil. Continue cooking over medium high heat until all the water has evaporated. Uncover and check the bottom of the potstickers. Each should be nice and golden brown. Serve with the brown side up with the following dip: 2 tbsp. light soy sauce, 1 tbsp. rice vinegar, and 1 tsp. sesame oil. Have hot oil with garlic on the side for those who like theirs hot.

Do-Ahead Notes: Wrap and freeze them. Cook just before serving. Add 5 more minutes to cooking time if they are frozen. (That means add a little more water in the beginning.)

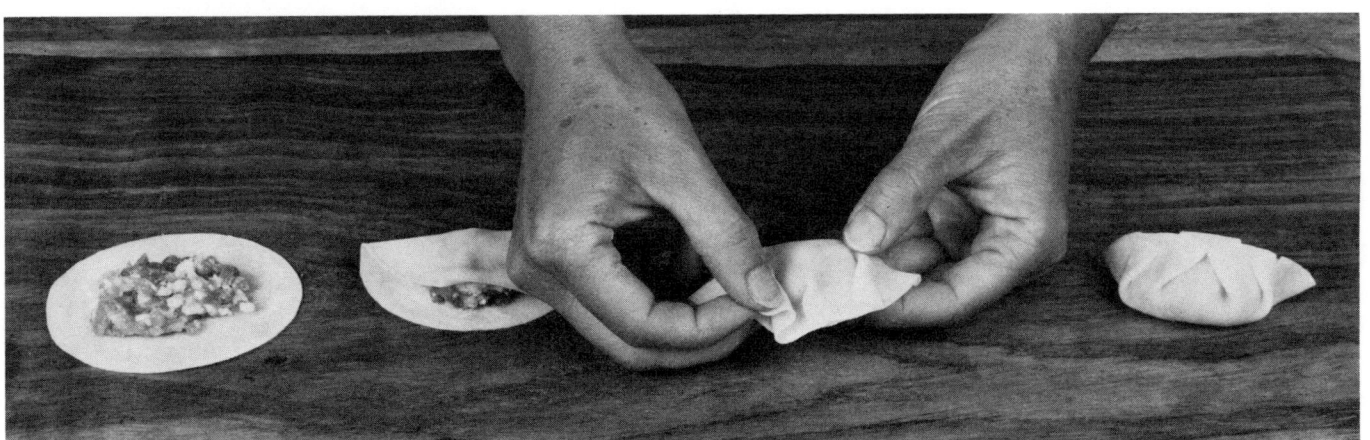

CHINESE CABBAGE IN CREAM SAUCE

Yield: Serves 4
- 1 Chinese cabbage (napa cabbage), about 2 lb.
- 1½ tbsp. cornstarch
- ½ cup cold milk
- 3 tbsp. rendered chicken fat
- 1 tsp. salt
- 1 tsp. sugar
- ¾ cup chicken stock

Preparation: Wash and cut cabbage into 1-inch slices. Combine cornstarch and milk.

Cooking: Stir fry cabbage in 2 tbsp. rendered chicken fat until all pieces are well coated with the fat. Add salt and sugar and continue to stir fry until cabbage is done, about 3 minutes. (The cabbage remains crunchy, but the raw taste disappears.) Drain cabbage well in a strainer. Transfer to serving dish. To the liquid left in the wok, add chicken stock with 1 tbsp. chicken fat and bring to a boil. Add the cornstarch/milk mixture and cook until thickened. Mix half of the sauce with cabbage, pour the rest over cabbage and serve.

Do-Ahead Notes: Do through preparation several hours in advance.

Comments: This is an exquisite vegetarian delight. It's a marvelous contrast to hot and spicy dishes, and it's delicious to serve with an all-meat dish such as smoked duck, or smoked chicken. The sauce should be snowy white and medium thick. Don't stir fry vegetables on high heat because the rendered fat may burn. If this happens, the liquid will have a light brown overcast and the sauce won't be as white.

STUFFED CUCUMBER RINGS

Yield: Serves 4
- 2-3 cucumbers

Filling mixture:
- 1 whole chicken breast, finely minced
- 2 tbsp. fat back (fresh pork fat), finely minced
- 1 egg white
- 1 tbsp. ice water
- 1 tbsp. cornstarch
- ½ tsp. salt
- ¼ tsp. sugar
- ⅛ tsp. white pepper

- 1 large carrot, about the same diameter as cucumbers

Chinese parsley

Sauce mixture:
- ½ cup chicken broth
- 2 tsp. cornstarch
- ¼ tsp. sesame oil
- ¼ tsp. sugar

Preparation: Combine filling mixture. Peel cucumbers and carrots. Cut 25 thin rounds from the carrot's wide end. Cut 25 1-inch rounds from the cucumbers. Hollow out the inside. Parboil carrots 3 to 4 minutes and cucumbers for 1½ to 2 minutes. Stuff cucumber rings with meat mixture. Oil a 10-inch round plate. Arrange carrot discs on the plate. Place a stuffed cucumber ring on top of each disc. Top each with a small Chinese parsley leaf. Combine sauce ingredients.

Cooking: Place the plate on a steamer rack and bring water to a boil. Cover and steam over medium heat for 10 minutes. Meanwhile, cook sauce in a small pan, stirring constantly until just thickened. Spoon sauce over steamed cucumber rings just before serving.

Do-Ahead Notes: Do through preparation and cook the sauce several hours in advance. While the stuffed cucumbers are being steamed, the sauce can be reheated on a slow burner without supervision.

Comments: The filling may be minced in a food processor with the fat back. The fat definately adds a sweeter taste and smoother texture to the filling. Another filling can be made by substituting fish, shrimp, or a combination of both for the chicken. For another variation, use dried Chinese mushrooms instead of carrot rounds. Soak them for 1 hour, squeeze dry, discard stems and arrange on a plate with the inner side facing up. Then proceed as before.

SOME LIKE IT SWEET AND SOUR

Sweet and sour dishes should never be served as the sole entree on any menu. This is one flavor that loses its effectiveness unless it's contrasted with another, opposite flavor, preferably salty, hot, or spicy. It is common practice in Chinese banquets to serve the sweet and sour dish towards the end of the dinner. By then the diners, having indulged in various courses of richly flavored foods, will be ready to appreciate the change to a lighter, sometimes fruity dish.

SWEET AND SOUR PORK SHANGHAI

Yield: Serves 4

¾ lb. pork butt, cut into ¾-inch cubes
Meat marinade:
    1 tbsp. Kikkoman soy sauce
    1 tbsp. sherry
    2 tsp. cornstarch
    2 tsp. flour
½ cup cornstarch
3-4 cups oil for deep frying
Sauce mixture:
    3 tbsp. oil
    4 tbsp. sugar
    4 tbsp. Chinese black vinegar
    4 tbsp. water
    2 tbsp. sherry
    1 tbsp. sesame oil
    4 tbsp. Kikkoman soy sauce
    2 tbsp. fresh lemon juice
    1 tsp. salt
    2 tbsp. garlic, minced
    1 green onion, minced
    2 tsp. cornstarch mixed with 2 tsp. water

Preparation: Marinate meat for about 2 hours, then dredge with cornstarch. Mix sauce ingredients.

Cooking: Heat oil in wok. Deep fry pork cubes in small batches until done, about 3 to 4 minutes for each batch. They'll turn a deep reddish-brown color. Meanwhile, cook sauce ingredients in a separate wok for 3 minutes, stirring occasionally. Add cornstarch/water mixture to slightly thicken the sauce. Add the deep fried pork, mix well, garnish with green onions and serve.

Do-Ahead Notes: Cook sauce and deep fry pork several hours in advance. Just before serving, reheat sauce on top of stove. Reheat pork cubes in preheated 400° oven for 6 to 7 minutes or deep fry quickly to crisp them.

Comments: This sweet and sour dish is quite different from the Cantonese style with its red sauce. This sauce is a deep, rich brown and its unique taste is due partly to the Chinese black vinegar. If you can't find black vinegar, substitute rice vinegar.

I first tasted this dish prepared by Chef Lee from

the Jien Jiang Hotel in Shanghai. He retired, moved to California and was keeping himself busy working part time in a local restaurant when I first met him. This is one of his specialities, but he wouldn't give me the recipe. I had to return time and time again to sample the dish, then return home to try and duplicate the taste. It was one of my most pleasurable self-assigned tasks.

YU HSIANG PORK

Yield: Serves 4

¾ lb. pork butt, cut the size of match sticks
4-5 wood ears, soaked for 1 hour
¾ cup bamboo shoots, cut the size of matchsticks

Meat marinade:
2 tsp. cornstarch
2 tsp. Kikkoman soy sauce
1 tsp. sesame oil
1 tsp. sherry

Sauce mixture:
2 tbsp. Kikkoman soy sauce
2 tbsp. Chinese black vinegar
1 tbsp. white vinegar
1 tbsp. hot bean sauce
1 tbsp. sugar
1 tsp. hot chili oil
1 tsp. sesame oil
2 tbsp. garlic, minced
2 tsp. cornstarch
2 green onions, chopped
3 cups oil

Preparation: Cut off ends of the soaked wood ear. Slice to the size of match sticks. Mix meat with marinade. Heat oil to just above the warm stage. Add pork mixture and stir to separate. Take out after ½ minute and drain well. Combine sauce ingredients.

Cooking: Heat 2 tbsp. oil in wok until hot. Stir fry wood ear and bamboo shoots for ½ minute. Add pork and sauce mixture. Stir until thickened and add green onions.

Do-Ahead Notes: Do through preparation several hours in advance.

Comments: This dish is both sour and hot. You may want to adjust the vinegar, sugar and hot bean sauce to suit your taste. If you prefer not to deep fry the pork strips, simply stir fry them with the wood ear. The reason for deep frying (velveting) is to make the pork's texture tender and smooth. If black vinegar is not available, use rice vinegar.

PINEAPPLE-LEMON CHICKEN

Yield: Serves 4

2 lb. chicken thighs or drumsticks
1 medium onion
Sauce mixture:
1 tbsp. lemon paste (see page 35)
1 tbsp. Kikkoman soy sauce
1 tbsp. sugar
2 tbsp. water
Juice from one 8 oz. can pineapple chunks
2 tbsp. fresh lemon juice
One 8 oz. can pineapple chunks
1 tsp. cornstarch mixed with 1 tsp. water

Preparation: Chop chicken into 1-inch pieces, bones and all. Slice onion into thin rings. Combine sauce ingredients.

Cooking: In a heavy casserole or wok, brown onion rings and chicken with 1 tbsp. oil. Add sauce mixture, cover, and cook over medium low heat for 20 minutes. Turn off heat and let chicken stand in the sauce for 4 to 6 hours, turning pieces over several times so each will be completely immersed. Reheat chicken quickly over medium high heat, adding the pineapple chunks and cornstarch/water mixture to thicken.

Do-Ahead Notes: Do through cooking several hours in advance and reheat just before serving.

Comments: Some lemon recipes I've tasted are too overpowering, often so sour my lips pucker. This one

is different. The sauce has a delicious, subtle lemon flavor due to the well-aged lemon paste with its lovely, distinctive flavor.

PLUM SAUCE CHICKEN

Yield: Serves 4

    2 whole chicken breasts, boned and cut in half
    Coating mixture:
        ½ cup flour
        ½ cup cornstarch
    1 egg, beaten
    1 cup pineapple chunks
    4-6 slices pineapple
    8-12 maraschino cherries
    1 tbsp. sesame seeds, toasted
    Sauce mixture:
        ¾ cup plum sauce
        2 tbsp. sugar
        ⅓ cup pineapple juice
        1 tbsp. white vinegar

Preparation: Cut pineapple slices in half. Combine sauce ingredients. Lightly salt chicken breasts, dip in beaten egg, then in coating mixture.

Cooking: Brown chicken breasts on both sides in a medium hot skillet with 1 to 2 tbsp. oil. While chicken is browning, heat sauce ingredients in a small pan. Cut cooked chicken breasts into 1-inch by 2-inch pieces and arrange on a small platter. Garnish with pineapple chunks. Surround the chicken pieces with halved pineapple slices and place one cherry in each curve of the slice. Pour heated sauce over chicken pieces and sprinkle with toasted sesame seeds.

Do-Ahead Notes: Do through preparation several hours in advance.

Comments: This is a most unusual dish. It's sweet and sour with a slightly spicy aftertaste.

LEMON CHICKEN

Yield: Serves 4

2 whole chicken breasts, boned
Salt
¾-1 cup cornstarch
⅓ cup oil
Sauce mixture:
    3 tbsp. fresh lemon juice
    3 tbsp. sugar
    1½ tsp. light soy sauce
    ½ tsp. sesame oil
    1 tbsp. oil
    ¼ tsp. salt
    ⅓ cup chicken broth
    2 tbsp. water
    2½ tsp. cornstarch
4-5 lemon slices, very thinly sliced
2 cups iceberg lettuce, coarsely shredded

Preparation: Cut chicken in half. Place skin side down and pound lightly so each half is the same thickness. Lightly sprinkle both sides with salt. Pat ½ cup cornstarch on both sides of each half. Let stand for several minutes so the cornstarch adheres to the chicken. Add more cornstarch, if necessary. Let stand for at least 15 minutes or keep in refrigerator overnight. Check next morning to see if more cornstarch is needed. Combine sauce ingredients.

Cooking: Cook sauce mixture, stirring constantly until thickened. Taste for sourness and adjust to your liking. Heat ⅓ cup oil in a 10-inch skillet and brown breasts on both sides until lightly golden. Drain on paper towel and cut into ½-inch wide strips. Arrange on serving platter on top of shredded lettuce. Pour sauce over top and garnish with lemon slices.

Do-Ahead Notes: Sauce can be cooked in advance and reheated. Chicken can be pan-fried in advance and reheated in a 400° oven for 5 minutes.

Comments: There are hundreds of ways to make lemon chicken. I think this is one of the easiest and tastiest.

RED GINGER CHICKEN

Yield: Serves 4

6 chicken thighs, skinned, boned, and diced into ½-inch cubes
Meat marinade:
    2 tsp. Kikkoman soy sauce
    1 tsp. cornstarch
    1 tsp. sherry
    1 egg white
Sauce mixture:
    2 tbsp. Kikkoman soy sauce
    1 tbsp. water
    2 tbsp. sugar
    2 tsp. rice vinegar
    2 tsp. cornstarch
    2 tsp. juice from a jar of shredded red ginger
    2 tbsp. red ginger, minced
2 tbsp. garlic, minced
3 tbsp. oil

Preparation: Mix cubed chicken with marinade. Combine sauce ingredients.

Cooking: Heat 3 tbsp. oil in wok until hot. Add garlic and chicken and stir fry until just done, about 2 to 3 minutes. Add sauce mixture and stir until thickened. Serve.

Do-Ahead Notes: Do through preparation several hours in advance.

Comments: The unique flavor of this dish comes from the shredded red ginger, available in jars in Chinatown. if you can't find red ginger, substitute 2 dried red chili peppers or fresh chili peppers, but be sure to thinly slice them. Also, add an extra teaspoon of rice vinegar to the sauce mixture to compensate for the lack of red ginger juice.

SWEET AND SOUR FISH

Yield: Serves 4

   One 1½-2 lb. red rock cod
   ½ cup carrots, cut into julienne strips
   ½ cup bamboo shoots, cut into julienne strips
   ½ cup green onion, cut into julienne strips
   ½ cup pickled red ginger
   ¼ cup fresh ginger, cut into julienne strips
Sauce mixture:
   ½ cup brown sugar
   ⅓ cup rice vinegar
   3 tbsp. catsup
   2 tbsp. Kikkoman soy sauce
   2 tbsp. water
   1 tsp. salt
   1 tbsp. cornstarch
3-4 cups oil

Preparation: Have the fish scaled and cleaned at the market. Make ½-inch deep scores, 3 to 4 times diagonally from the top to the belly on both sides.

Stand the fish on its belly and hit the back with the flat side of a cleaver. The belly will spread open further and it'll appear to be in a natural swimming position without any props. Sprinkle salt over entire fish and dredge with cornstarch. Cook sauce ingredients in a small pan. Add all vegetables to the sauce except green onions. Add onions just before serving.

Cooking: Heat oil in wok until hot. Deep fry fish for 5 to 6 minutes on one side. Turn over and fry another 3 to 4 minutes. It's done when you can insert a chopstick through the thickest part without resistance. Drain and place fish in an upright position. Add green onions to the heated sauce and pour over fish. Garnish with fresh Chinese parsley.

Do-Ahead Notes: Do through preparation several hours in advance and keep refrigerated.

Comments: This is a visually spectacular dish that tastes as good as it looks. Its unique taste comes from the shredded pickled ginger which gives a spicy flavor to an otherwise standard sauce. The sauce should be thick and smooth.

   I specified red rock cod because it's less expensive than the black rock cod the Chinese usually use for steaming. Fish steaks or fillets can be substituted for the whole fish.

SIZZLING SHRIMP PLATTER

Yield: **Serves 4**

    24 medium shrimp, shelled, cleaned and deveined
    1 small green pepper
    1 small onion

    Sauce mixture:
        2 tbsp. rice vinegar
        2 tbsp. brown sugar
        2 tbsp. pineapple or orange juice
        3 tbsp. catsup
        1 tbsp. plum sauce
        ½ tsp. salt
        1 tbsp. sherry
        1½ tsp. cornstarch
    2 cloves garlic, thinly sliced
    1 tbsp. fresh ginger, cut into thin strips
    2 cups cooked rice
    2 cups oil

Preparation: Press cooked rice into a ½-inch thick layer in a pie pan. Bake in 200° oven for 10 to 12 hours until hard and completely dried. Keep in air tight container until ready to use. (This will keep for several days.) Combine sauce ingredients. Cut green pepper into small cubes and onion into small wedges.

Cooking: In wok, heat 2 cups oil for deep frying the rice. As that is heating, in another wok, add 2 tbsp. oil and stir fry pepper and onion for 2 minutes. Remove from wok and set aside. Add 2 tbsp. oil and stir fry shrimp with garlic and ginger. Sprinkle ¾ tsp. salt into the shrimp. When shrimp turns pink, add sauce mixture. Keep warm. By now, the oil should be hot enough to deep fry the dried rice. Take rice out as soon as it puffs up. Transfer rice to a platter. Pour hot shrimp mixture over the rice and listen to it snap, crackle and pop!

Do-Ahead Notes: Do through preparation.

Comments: When you serve this dish, bring the fried rice to the table on the serving platter and the shrimp mixture in a separate bowl. Add the shrimp at the table so your audience can fully experience the sight, sound and wonderful aroma.

THE CHINESE GOLD RUSH

    The Cantonese, Chinese from the Southern part of the country, migrated to the United States during California's Gold Rush, and later played an important part in the construction of the Continental Railroad. They're a short, wiry, hard working lot. Their intentions were to work in the United States for a few years, then retire in China as rich men. What they earned in one year here was more than they'd make in several years at home. The Cantonese returning home from overseas spoke glowingly of the wonderful opportunities available to anyone willing to work. It was so easy getting a job and earning good money; it was like picking golden nuggets off the street. That's why the Cantonese still call America "Gum Sahn", the "Golden Mountain".

GOLDEN MOUNTAIN NUGGETS

Yield: **3 dozen nuggets**
    Dough:
        1 cup brown sugar
        ¼ cup hot water
        2¾ cups self-rising flour
        1¼ cup cooked sweet potato, mashed

Filling:
½ cup brown sugar
½ cup granulated sugar
½ cup coconut flakes
½ cup roasted peanuts, chopped

Preparation: Mix brown sugar with hot water. Add to flour and mix well. Knead in the mashed sweet potato until dough is soft and pliable. Oil your hands lighty if the dough gets too sticky.

Wrapping: Pinch off a small piece of dough, about the size of a walnut, and pat out into a 2-inch round of flat dough. Spoon 1 tsp. filling into the middle of the round and pinch dough to enclose. Roll between hands to form a ball. Continue making nuggets until all ingredients are used.

Cooking: Heat 3 cups of oil in wok on medium high heat. Deep fry nuggets for several minutes until golden brown. Drain on paper towel. Cool slightly and eat them while they're still warm.

Comments: The nuggets reheat beautifully in a preheated 425° oven for 5 to 6 minutes. For a savory snack, use the same amount of self-rising flour, but substitute 1¼ cup mashed white potato for the sweet potato. Mix the two ingredients with ½ cup plus 2 tbsp. chicken broth for the dough. Then use my *Dim Sum* Cookbook to make savory fillings such as curry beef or barbecue pork, or invent one yourself. Deep fry as directed above.

GLAZED APPLES

Yield: Serves 6 to 8

2 medium golden or red delicious apples
Juice from 1 lemon
Batter:
¼ cup Bisquick
¼ cup cornstarch
1 medium egg
2 tbsp. water
2 cups oil

Sugar glaze:
1 tbsp. oil
1 cup sugar
⅓ cup water

Preparation: Peel and core apples. Cut each into 8 equal slices. Mix batter. Brush apple slices with lemon juice and dip in batter. Deep fry in hot oil for 1 to 1½ minutes. Drain on paper towel. Drain off all but 1 tbsp. oil from the wok.

Cooking: Preheat oven at 400° and keep apple slices hot while you cook the sugar glaze. Heat the 1 tbsp. oil left in wok over fairly high flame and add sugar glaze mixture, stirring occasionally. Have a bowl of ice water at hand. The glaze is ready when a drop of it forms a hard ball instantly when dropped into the ice water. Take glaze off heat and immediately add hot apple slices. Mix quickly and drop the batch into the bowl of ice water. The apple slices will harden instantly. Serve 2 to 3 slices per person.

Do-Ahead Notes: Do through preparation several hours in advance.

Comments: This is a well-known Northern Chinese dessert. The hot apple slices encased in the cold, hardened sugar glaze offer delightful contrasts in taste and texture.

There are several critical steps to follow for success with this recipe:
• The batter must be fairly thick so the apple is completely encased, insuring it remains hot when dipped into the ice water. Make sure the apples have been in the oven for at least 10 minutes before glazing so they're good and hot.
• Use either the red or golden delicious apples because they're sweeter than other varieties.
• The cooking time for this amount of sugar glaze in a 12-inch wok is about 9 to 9½ minutes before it begins to reach the proper "hard crack" stage. I don't use a candy thermometer because I've always been a "sight and feel" cook. Start testing after about 7 minutes of cooking. Once the sugar has reached the "hard crack" stage, take it off the heat immediately. It

doesn't take long before it gets to the "burnt" stage. and tastes bitter. This is the most critical point of the recipe, so don't be disappointed if you don't succeed the first time. When you get this down to a science, it's easy.

APPLE CRISPIES WE-NAT-CHEE

Yield: Four 4-inch apple crispies

⅔ cup flour
¼ cup warm water
½-¾ cup apples, finely chopped
1 tsp. lemon juice
Butter or margarine, softened
4 tbsp. brown sugar
4 tsp. granulated sugar
Cinnamon
Nutmeg

Preparation: Mix flour with water and knead for 5 minutes. Let rest for 15 minutes. Sprinkle lemon juice over chopped apples and mix well.

To Make Apple Crispies: Separate dough into 4 equal portions. Roll one portion out to a 4-inch to 5-inch round (as thin as possible) and spread a thin layer of softened butter or margarine onto it. Sprinkle ¼ of the chopped apples, 1 tbsp. brown sugar and 1 tsp. granulated sugar over the buttered dough. Sprinkle lightly with cinnamon and nutmeg. Roll up dough jelly roll style, then coil it around in snail fashion, tucking the end under. Roll out again to a 4-inch round. Continue in the same manner with the other 3 pieces of dough.

Cooking: Heat a 6-inch to 8-inch skillet on medium heat with 1 tbsp. oil. Brown each apple crispy on both sides until golden. Drain on paper towel. Cut each crispy into quarters with scissors and enjoy them while hot.

Do-Ahead Notes: The rolled crispies can be kept frozen between waxed paper for about 1 month. Thaw overnight in the refrigerator before cooking.

Comments: This recipe is for all the wonderful friends I made when I taught at Pat Kealoha's Red Rose Cooking School in Wenatchee, Washington, the apple country. Among many other momentos, I was given a beautiful box of apples to bring home. I promised I'd try to create an apple recipe just for them. Here it is and now we can all enjoy it. The treats are crunchy, flaky and crispy. Terrific with coffee, tea, or vanilla-based ice cream.

SOME LIKE IT WILD

My friend Don Linck is a sharp shooter and an avid sportsman. Each hunting season you'll find him bringing home all kinds of wild game; and his freezer is crammed with duck, venison, mourning dove and quail. Don's wife, Linda, a versatile and creative cook, is always searching for new ideas and trying out new recipes for wild game.

One day Don and Linda asked me if I'd like to try cooking some game *a la Chinoise.* I must admit I didn't have much experience with wild meats but the idea intrigued me, so I accepted the challenge. The following recipes were some of the dishes we had one evening when I took my "wok on the wild side."

VENISON STEW

Yield: Serves 6 to 8

- 2 lb. venison
- 5-6 cloves garlic, mashed
- 1 chunk fresh ginger, size of a half dollar, mashed
- 1 cup chicken broth
- ¼ cup Kikkoman soy sauce
- ½ cup catsup
- 4 medium white potatoes, peeled
- 8-10 carrots, peeled
- 1 large onion
- 3 medium zucchini
- 3-4 stalks celery
- 3 tbsp. oil

Preparation: Cut venison and all vegetables into 1-inch cubes.

Cooking: In a 4-quart casserole or heavy pot, heat oil with garlic and ginger. Brown venison on all sides. Add chicken broth, soy sauce and catsup. Cover and cook over medium heat until tender, about 45 minutes to 1 hour. Check liquid for evaporation and add more broth if necessary. Uncover and add carrots, potatoes, onion, celery and 1 tsp. salt. Mix well with meat and continue cooking for 20 minutes. Add zucchini and cook 15 minutes more. Make sure the contents of the casserole are half covered with liquid. Otherwise add more broth, soy sauce and catsup in proportionate amounts. Adjust seasoning, if necessary.

Do-Ahead Notes: This stew tastes much better the next day after other flavors have a chance to penetrate the potatoes and zucchini. Refrigerate overnight. Take out the next morning and let stand at room temperature most of the day. Reheat on medium low heat so the bottom of the pot won't scorch.

Comments: Try this recipe on beef stew meat, oxtails or beef ribs with or without bones. Oxtails will require a longer cooking time, but the meat definitely is more tender and smoother than either beef stew meat or venison. Cook the oxtails in a pressure cooker for 15 minutes over medium high heat. After the pressure goes down, cook the vegetables without pressure as in the recipe. Great over rice!

For a slightly different flavor, add ¼ cup hoisin sauce and 2 tbsp. sugar to the cooking sauce. For a mildly spicy flavor, add 1 tsp. Szechwan peppercorns (to start) and ½ tsp. white pepper. If you like it really spicy hot, add crushed dried chili pepper in addition to the above spices. Start with 2 tsp.

SPICY VENISON

Yield: Serves 6 to 8

1 lb. venison
Meat marinade:
    1½ tbsp. Kikkoman soy sauce
    2 tsp. sherry
    1 tbsp. cornstarch
    2 tsp. oil
    A few dashes white pepper
Sauce mixture:
    2 tbsp. fresh ginger, minced
    2 tbsp. garlic, minced
    2 tbsp. hot bean sauce
    2 tbsp. sweet bean sauce
    2 tbsp. Kikkoman soy sauce
    2 tbsp. sherry
    1 tsp. rice vinegar
    2 tsp. sugar
    1 tsp. cornstarch
1 large green pepper, cubed
1 medium onion, cut into small wedges
4-5 whole dried red chili peppers
4 tbsp. oil

Preparation: Cut venison cross-grain into thin slices. Mix with meat marinade for ½ hour. Combine sauce ingredients.

Cooking: Heat wok. Add 1 tbsp. oil and stir fry green pepper with onion wedges for 2 minutes, adding a little salt to taste and ¼ tsp. sugar. Set aside. Add 2-3 tbsp. oil and add whole chili peppers. Let cook for 20 seconds and add venison. Stir fry until venison is just done, about 2 minutes. Add sauce and stir until thickened. Add back the vegetables.

Do-Ahead Notes: Do through preparation.

Comments: I treat venison like flank steak. When thinly sliced and quickly cooked, it becomes juicy and tender. You might try substituting venison in other flank steak recipes.

RED COOK WILD DUCKS

Yield: Serves 2

2 wild ducks
Red cook sauce:
    1 cup dark soy sauce
    ½ cup Kikkoman soy sauce
    ½ cup thin soy sauce
    1 cup sherry
    1 cup water
    1 star anise
    1 cup sugar
    ½ tsp. five spice powder
    6-8 cloves garlic, mashed
    1 chunk fresh ginger, size of a silver dollar, mashed
    1 stalk leek or 3-4 green onions, cut into 1-inch lengths
4 tsp. cornstarch
1 cup red cook sauce
2 green onions, chopped

Cooking: Bring red cook sauce mixture to a boil and add ducks. When the sauce returns to a boil, lower heat and simmer birds gently until done, about 30 to 40 minutes. If sauce is not covering ducks completely, turn them over several times while cooking to insure even coloring.

    Chop duck into 2-inch pieces and arrange on a serving platter. Take 1 cup of sauce and cook with 4 tsp. cornstarch until thickened. Pour over duck and garnish with chopped green onions.

Do-Ahead Notes: Cook ducks ½ hour before serving. You may chop them as soon as they're cool enough to handle. Make sauce several hours in advance and reheat just before serving. The amount of sauce depends on the size of the ducks. Don't drown the birds.

Comments: Quail and squab also can be cooked this way. On the domestic side, game hens are succulent and tender using this recipe. Game hens require only 15 minutes of simmering.

BREAST OF MOURNING DOVE IN HOISIN SAUCE

Yield: Serves 4

8-10 mourning dove breasts
Meat marinade:
    1 tbsp. cornstarch
    1 tbsp. Kikkoman soy sauce
    1 tbsp. sherry
    1 tsp. sesame oil
8-10 medium fresh mushrooms, quartered
1 cup bamboo shoots, cut into ½-inch cubes
3 tbsp. fresh ginger, minced
3 tbsp. garlic, minced
4 green onions, cut into ½-inch lengths
1 tbsp. sherry
1 tsp. sugar
Sauce mixture:
    1 tbsp. catsup
    2 tbsp. hoisin sauce
    2 tbsp. sweet bean sauce
    ⅓ cup chicken broth
    1 tsp. sesame oil
3-4 tbsp. oil

Preparation: Cut dove breasts into thin slices. Mix with meat marinade for ½ hour. Combine sauce ingredients.

Cooking: Heat 2 tbsp. oil in wok and stir fry fresh mushrooms and bamboo shoots, adding 1 tbsp. sherry, 1 tsp. sugar, and salt to taste. Set aside. Heat remaining 2 tbsp. oil with minced garlic and ginger for 30 seconds. Add meat and stir fry until done, about 3 minutes. Add sauce mixture, then all vegetables including green onions. Mix well and serve.

Do-Ahead Notes: Do through preparation.

Comments: We were delighted with this dish. It was tender, tasty and not at all gamy.

NEVER WOK ALONE!

You've just finished your first series of Chinese cooking lessons and, now that your family is literally eating out of your hands, you're ready to entertain guests with your first Chinese dinner party.

Naturally, you want to impress everyone. So you decide on an elaborate menu following the Chinese custom advising "one dish per person plus one for the table." If you have eight people for dinner, you'll have to come up with nine dishes. Though that might not be too demanding for an experienced cook, it's an exhausting experience for someone still new to Chinese cooking.

Not to worry! Many options are available so you can have your Chinese egg roll and eat it too. The secret is my motto: NEVER WOK ALONE! That's right. Let your guests do the woking and your party will be the talk of the town. It'll be a fun-filled and unique learning experience for everyone involved.

The following are three "Wok-along" parties which can easily be set up in your home. It'll take a bit of preparation on your part, but once you're finished, the guests will take over. You just sit back and enjoy the compliments and kudos.

THE GREAT PANCAKE PARTY

The Northern Chinese have a delicious, flaky, crispy onion pancake that's absolutely out of this world. It's usually served as an appetizer, or as a side dish for lunch. I've found it's wonderful with soup or salad in place of bread.

Another favorite is Muu Shu Pork with Peking Doilies. These paper-thin pancakes are so called because they're as delicate as their name implies. They're used as wrappers for Muu Shu Pork, a stir fried filling made with pork strips and several kinds of dried and fresh vegetables. Once the filling is wrapped in the doilies, they're eaten immediately, much like Mexican burritos.

The basic dough for both pancakes and doilies is made with a flour and water base. Once the dough is prepared, let your guests make the onion pancakes by providing a variety of ingredients and seasonings.

For Muu Shu Pork, make the doilies in advance and keep hot in a steamer. Keep the cooked Muu Shu Pork warm on a hot plate. Guests help themselves by filling and wrapping their own "Chinese burritos".

All you'll need for accompaniment are any or all of the following soups or salads. What you choose depends on the size of the crowd, weather (soup on a cold day), and available space. One of my favorite soups is the Hot and Sour on page 27. Another is Chinese Congee or Joak on page 26. As for salads, try the Rainbow Salad on page 13 or the Spicy Chicken Salad on page 14. All four recipes are good fix-ahead dishes. A glass of your favorite wine and one or two non-alcoholic beverages such as sparkling cider or tea will round out the menu.

For dessert, don't forget Apples We-nat-chee (page 72). Your guests can make them, too.

ONION PANCAKES

Yield: 8 to 10 4-inch pancakes

1⅓ cup flour
½ cup warm water
4 stalks green onions, chopped
½ cup dried onion flakes
Shortening
Seasoned salt
½ cup oil

Preparation: Soak dried onion flakes for 10 minutes. Drain. Mix with chopped green onions.

To Make Pancakes: Mix flour with water and knead for 5 minutes. Let rest for 10 to 15 minutes. Separate into 8 to 10 parts and roll each into a flat 4-inch round. Spread a thin layer of shortening on the dough and sprinkle with seasoned salt and 1 tbsp. of the onion mixture. Roll up jelly roll style, then coil it around in snail fashion, tucking ends under. Roll out again to a 4-inch round. See demonstration photos of Apple Crispies on page 72.

Cooking: Heat skillet on medium heat and add 1 tbsp. oil. Brown onion pancakes slowly on both sides until golden. Serve hot.

Do-Ahead Notes: Rolled out pancakes can be frozen between layers of waxed paper 2 to 3 weeks in advance. Thaw overnight in the refrigerator. Brown just before serving.

Comments: You can roll out pancakes in advance if you don't have available work space for a lot of people. Then the guests will just cook their own pancakes. But the fun really is letting them make their own, adding some of the following ingredients for variations.

Variations: Add one or more of the following to the basic dough*:

3-4 strips bacon, fried and crumbled
1 Chinese sausage, thinly sliced
½ cup fresh onion, minced (instead of dried onion flakes)
1-2 tbsp. curry powder
1-2 tbsp. five spice powder
1-2 tbsp. red chili powder
1-2 tbsp. sesame seeds, toasted
1-2 tbsp. salted turnips, minced
1-2 tbsp. Szechwan pickled mustard, minced

*The above amounts are for one basic recipe of 8 to 10 pancakes.

MUU SHU PORK

Yield: Fills 12 to 14 small doilies, 4-inch to 4½-inches round

½ lb. pork, cut the size of match sticks
Meat marinade:
  1 tsp. cornstarch
  2 tsp. dark soy sauce
  1 tsp. sherry
4 dried Oriental mushrooms
24 lily buds
¼ cup cloud ears
1 cup bean sprouts
1 cup bamboo shoots, cut the size of match sticks
2 cups napa cabbage, shredded
2 green onions, cut into ½-inch lengths
Sauce mixture:
  1 tbsp. cornstarch
  1 tbsp. sherry
  2 tbsp. oyster sauce
  1 tsp. light soy sauce
  1 tsp. sesame oil
  ¼ cup chicken broth
2 tbsp. oil
¼ cup hoisin sauce
Onion brushes (see Preparation)

Preparation: Mix pork with meat marinade for ½ hour. Soak mushrooms, lily buds and cloud ears until soft. Discard mushroom stems and cut caps into thin slices. Tie a knot in the middle of each lily bud and nip off tough ends. Pinch off tough parts of cloud ears and break into small pieces. Combine sauce ingredients.

Make onion brushes by cutting the white part of green onions into 3-inch lengths. Make several ½-inch lengthwise cuts on both ends. Soak in ice water for a few hours. The cut ends will flare out like brushes.

Cooking: Stir fry bean sprouts in 1 tsp. oil for 1 minute. Set aside. Add 2 tsp. oil and stir fry bamboo shoots with cabbage for 2 to 2½ minutes. Set aside. Add 1 tbsp. oil and stir fry pork, mushrooms, lily buds and cloud ears until pork is done, about 2 to 3 minutes. Add sauce mixture, stirring until thickened. Add back vegetables including the green onions. Serve with Peking Doilies (next recipe).

To Serve: Spread a little hoisin sauce on a doily with the tip of the onion brush and spoon on Muu Shu Pork. Wrap and eat as a finger food.

Do-Ahead Notes: Muu Shu Pork can be made ahead and kept warm for ½ hour.

PEKING DOILIES

Yield: 18 doilies

    2 cups all purpose flour, sifted
    ½ cup plus 4 tsp. boiling water
    Sesame oil (or vegetable oil)

Preparation: Mix boiling water with flour and knead for 10 minutes. Let dough rest for 10 minutes. Break into 18 pieces. Roll each piece into a ball, then flatten with the heel of your hand. Brush half of the rounds with sesame or vegetable oil.

Top each with another, unoiled, round. Roll each double round into a 6 to 7-inch round.

Cooking: Heat a Teflon or heavy-bottomed skillet without oil over medium heat. Cook doilies for 1 minute or less on each side. They should turn a light beige. Cool for several seconds and separate doilies as soon as possible while still hot.

Do-Ahead Notes: These can be cooked in advance and frozen for 1 to 2 months. There is no need to separate them with waxed paper. Steam frozen doilies for 12 minutes or, if thawed, steam for 6 to 7 minutes.

Comments: The following points should be observed to make successful doilies:
• The dough should be a bit on the dry side. Not too dry or the doillies will crack, but definately not so soft that they become too mushy for rolling and separating.

- Oil the flattened dough well, especially the edges, in order to have an easier time pulling them apart.
- Roll doillies out and away from the center in one stroke in all directions to insure eveness and a round shape. Don't roll with a back and forth motion since the edges may fold in and they'll be difficult to separate.

Having a tortilla press would be a plus factor. Before you begin rolling the two doillies together (they're a bit slippery because of the oil in between), press them on the tortilla press. It'll help you get started much more quickly.

THE NOODLE PARTY

Noodles are one of the staffs of life in the Northern Chinese diet, but they're just as popular in Southern cuisine. As a matter of fact, I'll have noodles for dinner anytime. I'm sure I'm not the only one. There must be many other noodle freaks like me getting a fix of them once or twice a week.

Other people may get turned on by chocolate, ice cream or sweet desserts. Me? It's noodles and the whole pasta scene! One look at a plate of chow mein, chow fun, fettucine or spagetti, and my knees weaken, my salivary glands go into overtime, my taste buds yearn for that first bite and, throwing caution to the winds, I dive into that plate of noodles like there's no tomorrow. Ah!....Heaven!

The following recipes start with basic Chinese egg noodles which have been parboiled for about 3 minutes (al dente), then rinsed briefly under cold water. Now they're ready to combine with different seasonings and stir fried mixtures you'll provide for your guests. All they need to do is toss the noodles with their choice of seasonings.

For an accompaniment, the Spinach Salad (page 13) is good. You could also include Spicy Cucumbers (page 17) and chilled Braised Bamboo Shoots (pages 13-14) for greater selection. They're all do-ahead dishes that improve with at least 1 day's chilling in the refrigerator. Of course, you can use other salads in this book, or try some of your own.

JA JIANG MEIN

Yield: Serves 2 to 3

½ lb. egg noodles
½ lb. ground pork
1 cup cucumber, shredded
2-3 tbsp. bean sauce
2-3 cloves garlic, minced
¼ tsp. white pepper
¼ tsp. salt
½ tsp. sugar
2 tbsp. chicken broth or water
1 tbsp. oil

Preparation: Parboil noodles in 2 quarts boiling water with 3 tbsp. oil for 2 minutes. Rinse under cold water and drain well.

Cooking: Heat 1 tbsp. oil in wok. Brown pork with minced garlic and bean sauce until pork is done, about 1 to 2 minutes. Add remaining seasonings and water. Mix well. Divide noodles into 2 to 3 portions, depending on appetites. Place in soup bowls. Spoon pork mixture on one side of noodles and garnish other half with shredded cucumber. Serve.

Do-Ahead Notes: Do through cooking of pork mixture several hours in advance. Reheat mixture before serving and spoon over cold noodles.

Comments: This is another popular Northern dish

in which noodles are served chilled. If you want yours spicier, add ½ to 1 tsp. chili oil when stir frying.

DON DON NOODLES

Yield: Serves 2

⅔ lb. fresh egg noodles
Sauce Mixture:
 ¼ tsp. Szechwan peppercorns, finely ground
 2-3 tbsp. hot chili oil
 1-1½ tsp. peanut butter
 ⅛ tsp. MSG (optional)
 ½ tsp. sugar
 2 cloves garlic, minced
 1 green onion, minced
 3 tbsp. Kikkoman soy sauce

Preparation: Combine sauce mixture by mashing the first 3 ingredients, then adding the remainder.

Cooking: Cook noodles in 2 quarts boiling water until just done, about 2 minutes. Drain. Divide into 2 portions and place in bowls. Spoon half of sauce mixture into each bowl. Mix and serve.

Comments: The hotness depends on the strength of the chili oil. You may want to start out with 2 tsp. of the hot oil. You can always add more if you want it hotter. Add salad oil or sesame oil to make up the difference in the total amount of oil. Traditionally, this is a very hot dish.

NOODLES WITH SHREDDED PORK AND PICKLED MUSTARD GREENS

Yield: Serves 4

1½ cup pickled mustard greens, shredded
1½ cup pork, cut into thin strips
Meat marinade:
   2 tsp. Kikkoman soy sauce
   ½ tsp. sesame oil
   1 tsp. cornstarch
   1 tsp. sherry
1 green onion, minced
1 tbsp. oil
1 lb. fresh egg noodles

Preparation: Mix pork with marinade. Cook noodles in 3 to 4 quarts boiling water for 2 minutes. Drain well.

Cooking: While waiting for water to come to a boil, stir fry pork with green onions and mustard greens. Keep warm. Have 4 bowls ready. In each bowl, put 1 tsp. each of Kikkoman soy sauce and sesame oil. Divide the cooked noodles into 4 portions and place in bowls. Toss well to mix. Add stir fried mixture to top.

Do-Ahead Notes: Do through preparation several hours in advance. To reheat noodles, place them in a bowl of hot water for 15 seconds. Drain well and proceed according to the recipe. Serve the noodles cold or at room temperature on hot summer days.

Comments: This is a common Northern style noodle dish. Pickled mustard greens are sold in plastic packages in Chinese grocery stores. To make them yourself, see page 36.
   For the noodle party, pre-cook noodles, drain well and have another pot of hot water simmering. Guests can help themselves and reheat noodles in the pot of simmering water. They can combine the noodles with the stir fried mixture for as long as the fixings last.

PORK LO MEIN

Yield: Serves 6 to 8

½ lb. fresh pork butt, cut the size of match sticks
Meat marinade:
   2 tsp. cornstarch
   1 tsp. sugar
   1 tbsp. light soy sauce
   1 tsp. sherry
2 tbsp. fresh ginger, slivered
4 dried Oriental mushrooms
½ cup bamboo shoots
1 red bell pepper
1 small onion, cut into small wedges
2 green onions, shredded and cut into 1-inch lengths
1 medium zucchini
Sauce mixture:
   4 tsp. cornstarch
   1 cup chicken broth
   2 tbsp. oyster sauce
2 cloves garlic, crushed
1 chunk ginger, size of a quarter, crushed
4 tbsp. oil
1 tsp. sugar
1 lb. fresh egg noodles
Seasonings for noodles:
   2 tbsp. oil
   1 tbsp. sesame oil
   2 tbsp. oyster sauce
   1½ tbsp. light soy sauce
   1½ tsp. vinegar

Preparation: Mix pork with meat marinade and let stand for ½ hour. Soak mushrooms until soft. Discard stems. Slice caps, bamboo shoots, red bell pepper and zucchini into thin strips. Combine sauce ingredients. Parboil noodles for 3 minutes. Rinse and drain. Bring another pot of water to boil and keep hot.

Cooking: Heat 2 tbsp. oil in wok and stir fry all the vegetables together for 2 to 3 minutes. Sprinkle on a little salt and 1 tsp. sugar. Set aside. Add 2 tbsp. oil

and brown crushed garlic and ginger for 30 seconds. Discard garlic and ginger and add pork. Stir fry until done, about 2 to 3 minutes. Add sauce mixture, stirring until thickened. Add vegetables. Mix well and keep warm.

Put noodles back into hot water for 10 to 15 seconds, just to reheat. Drain but don't rinse. Put noodles back in empty pot and add noodle seasonings. Mix well. Transfer noodles to individual plates or bowls and add meat mixture to top.

Do-Ahead Notes: Prepare the stir fried mixture in advance and keep warm. Have a pot of hot water handy so guests can reheat noodles in any amount they desire. They can combine the noodles with the seasonings and add the topping.

THE CHINESE FONDUE PARTY

Here's a surefire dinner that'll win praise from even your most critical guests, since they do all the cooking. It's fondue, Chinese style. But instead of cooking the food in oil, its cooked in a simmering broth at the table. And wait until you drink the broth at the end of the meal after all the food has been simmered in it!

MONGOLIAN FIRE POT

Yield: Serves 6 to 8

½ lb. flank steak
½ lb. chicken breast
½ lb. fillet of fish (any kind)

½ lb. shrimp
1 small head Chinese cabbage
1 bunch spinach
2 squares bean cake
¼ lb. fresh mushrooms
½ lb. fresh egg noodles
Meat and seafood marinade (for each ½ lb.):
  2 tsp. sherry
  1 tsp. light soy sauce
  ½ tsp. sesame oil
3-4 quarts chicken stock

Preparation: Slice flank steak, chicken breasts, and fish fillets as thin as possible. Shell, devein and clean shrimp. Marinate each in separate bowls for 2 hours then arrange them together on small plates, one plate for each person.

Parboil noodles for 2 minutes, rinse and drain. Place in bowl. Wash and clean vegetables. Thinly slice mushrooms. Cut bean cake into 1-inch by ½-inch by ¼-inch pieces. Slice Chinese cabbage into 2-inch by 1-inch pieces. Keep spinach leaves whole.

Sauces and Condiments:
- Sweet mixed ginger: Slice contents of sweet mixed ginger into thin strips.
- Soy-vinegar dip: Mix 4 parts light soy sauce to 1 part vinegar.
- Oyster sauce dip: Mix 2 parts oyster sauce to 1 part dark soy sauce.
- Hot mustard dip: Mix Chinese mustard powder with water until it becomes a paste. Add a little salad oil for a smooth and shiny appearance.
- Plum sauce dip: Mix 4 parts canned plum sauce to 1 part sugar and 1 part rice vinegar.
- Hot oil dip: Mix 2 parts hot bean sauce to 1 part sweet bean sauce and 1 part hot oil.
- Hoisin sauce dip: Mix 1 tsp. hoisin sauce, 1 tbsp. catsup, ¼ tsp. vinegar, ½ tsp. sugar and ½ tsp. dark soy sauce.

Table Setting: Place small individual meat and seafood plates at upper left of each setting. Put dips and condiments in small soy sauce dishes directly above the setting. Center dinner plate. Place wire strainer at the left, chopsticks on the right. Place soup bowl with Chinese soup spoon at upper right, above chopsticks.

Table Top Cooking: Place the hot pot -- a round one is best -- in the middle of the dining table. Heat chicken stock to boiling. Each guest places a small amount of meat in the wire strainer and dips it into the boiling broth for 1 minute or less -- just enough time to heat it through. Then he dunks the cooked meat into any of the dips.

From time to time, the hostess should add the vegetables to the broth so guests can add these to their plates. The noodles usually are served at the end of the meal when they are added to the broth. Everyone eats the noodles and drinks the broth.

Do-Ahead Notes: Do through preparation several hours in advance.

Comments: This is a marvelous 1-dish meal, a favorite among Chinese families on cold, wintry nights. It's a leisurely way to dine with old friends, or a great ice breaker for new acquaintances, if you have someone on your dinner list whose cooking *always* intimidates you, this is the menu that'll give you self-confidence.

Have no more than 6 to a table, as 8 people crowd things. If you want to entertain more, it's better to have two small settings with 4 to each table.

GLOSSARY

Here is a list of ingredients common in Chinese cooking. For the sake of simplicity, it includes only those used in this book. All can be purchased from stores specializing in Oriental foods, although, with the increasing interest in Chinese cooking, some are now available in supermarkets.

ANISE, STAR: See star anise

BAMBOO SHOOTS: (juk soon) An ivory colored vegetable, usually available in cans, either whole or sliced. The unused portion can be kept for about 1 week in a jar, provided the water is changed each day to keep them from spoiling.

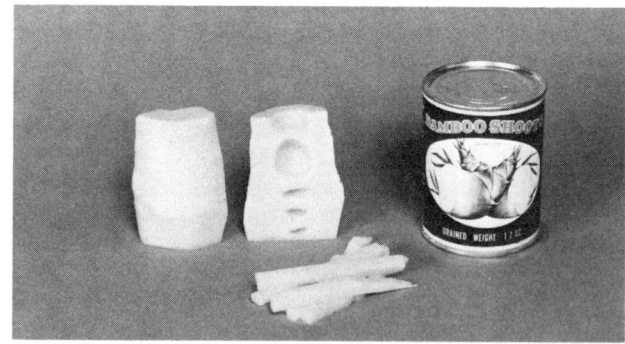

BEAN CAKE: (tofu or dow fu) Because it's made from soy beans, bean cake has a high protein content. It's an excellent food for babies since it digests easily. It's also good for children who don't care for meat. Bean cake has a smooth, creamy texture, a bland taste and readily absorbs the flavor of soups and sauces. it can be purchased fresh in produce sections or in cans. Fresh bean cake spoils easily and must be used within 1 or 2 days of purchase.

BEAN CURDS - WET: These small bean cakes, kept in glass jars, are 1-inch squares resembling cakes of fresh yeast. They are soaked in an alcohol-based liquid for several weeks before they're ready to eat. Good by themselves or as seasoning in certain dishes, they have a strong taste of alcohol and are fairly salty.

BEAN SAUCE: (mein see) Prepared from the residue left after making soy sauce, it's also called brown bean sauce, or soy bean condiment. It has a thick consistency, and is available in cans or jars. Bean sauce is used to flavor pork, fowl, bland vegetables and bean cake. The unused portion will keep for months in a refrigerated jar.

BEAN SAUCE - HOT: A thick, dark, reddish sauce with bits of soy beans flavored with chili peppers. It's spicy. Many brands are available, some in cans, some in jars. I've found that, generally, those in cans are milder then those in jars. This is used widely in Szechwan cooking.

BEAN SAUCE - SWEET: A thick, dark, reddish brown sauce made from soy beans, flour, sugar, pepper and bean sauce. It's used in meat dishes as a compliment to hoisin or hot bean sauce. It also tones down the hotness of chili peppers and imparts a faint trace of sweetness to other basic sauces.

BEAN SPROUTS: (nga choy) A vegetable grown from green mung peas. It has a 2-inch long white shoot with a small green hood. the texture is delicate and crunchy. Bean sprouts shouldn't be cooked for more than 1 minute, or they'll become limp and lose crispness. Fresh bean sprouts don't keep well and should be used as soon as possible.

BEAN THREAD: (fun see) Also called long rice or cellophane noodles. These are dry, thin, white noodles made from green mung peas. They puff up immediatley when dropped in hot oil. When used in other types of cooking, however, they must be soaked first. The noodles become transparent when cooked, thus the name, cellophane noodles.

BLACK BEANS: (dow see) Tiny, soft, extremely salty black beans used to season meat and sea food. They're washed, then mashed with fresh garlic and ginger. They can be stored at room temperature.

BOK CHOY: A leafy vegetable with white stalks and dark green leaves, it looks somewhat like Swiss chard, but the taste isn't as strong. Bok choy can be stir fried alone or with meat, and can be dropped into broth to make soup. It's also available dried, in small bunches. The dried variety is used mainly in soup.

CHILI OIL: Hot, red oil made from ground chili peppers mixed with heated salad oil. It's used for seasoning or as a dipping condiment.

CHILI PEPPERS - DRIED: Deep red and extremely hot, they can be stir fried whole or finely minced for use in sauces. They also can be purchased in powder form. They're used extensively in Szechwan cooking.

CHINESE CABBAGE: (wong bok or yea choy) A tall, tightly packed vegetable with wide, white stalks and yellow-green wrinkled leaves. It's delicious when cooked, and is one vegetable that actually tastes better overcooked. Used for soup or stir fry dishes.

CHINESE PARSLEY: (yuen sai) Also known as cilentro or coriander, this is a bright green herb with slender, delicate stems and small, serrated, flat leaves. It's highly aromatic, has a strong, pungent flavor and is used as a garnish or as a bouquet in roasting poultry.

CHINESE SAUSAGE: (lop cheung) These slender pork sausages come in pairs, each one 6-inches long. They're thinly sliced and can be cooked directly on top of rice, steamed separately, or steamed with bland meats. Stir fry them with any vegetable or use in rice stuffings. To store, wrap in plastic and freeze.

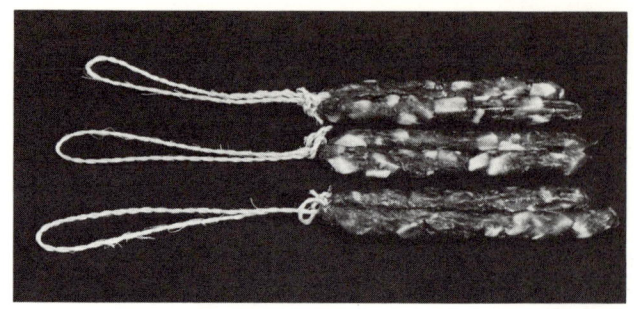

CILENTRO: See Chinese Parsley.

CLOUD EAR: (wan yee) A small, dried grayish-brown fungus about 1-inch long. It expands to several times its size when soaked. The texture is crunchy and delicate, and it's either steamed or used in stir fry dishes.

CORIANDER: See Chinese Parsley. Photo shows ground version.

DOW FU: See Bean Cake.

EGGPLANT, ORIENTAL: Small eggplant shaped like a blackjack. It tastes sweeter and cooks faster than the Western variety.

FISH - SALTED: Some are as tiny as 1-inch, others are 3 to 4 pounders. They're sold by the pound. Smaller ones must be soaked before steaming. Larger fish usually are steamed in small chunks either alone or with pork.

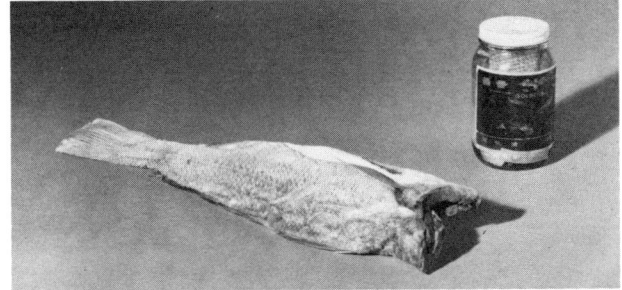

FIVE SPICE POWDER: (eng hung fun) A blend, in powder form, of star anise, cinnamon, cloves, fennel and anise pepper. It has a mustard color and is used in roasting meats and poultry.

GINGER, FRESH ROOT: (gueng) A gnarled, spicy, beige root that's a must in Chinese cooking. Never substitute ginger powder. It's better to leave ginger out completely if you don't have the fresh root on hand. It's especially good on sea food since it alleviates the fishy odor. Store by freezing or break it into small chunks and keep refrigerated in a jar filled with sherry. it also can be stored in a small plastic bag (opened) in a cool, dark place, much as potatoes are stored.

GINGER, SHREDDED RED: Pickled, julienne-sliced pinkish-red ginger sold in jars. Great for fish; it has a slightly hot-sour flavor.

GINGER, SWEET MIXED: Also known as *sub gum geung* or *sub gum* vegetables, this is canned or jarred sweet and sour ginger mixed with vegetables. It can be used as a garnish or chilled and eaten as a relish.

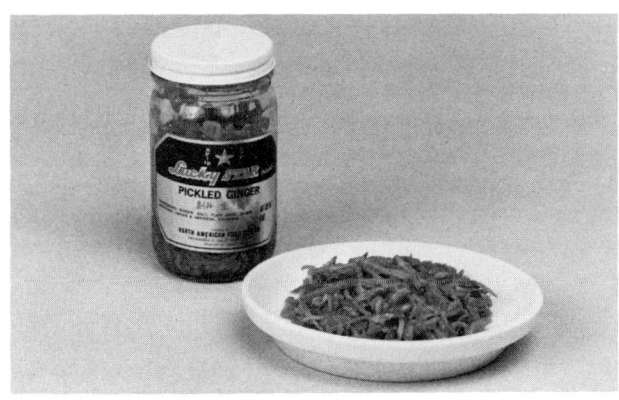

GLUTINOUS RICE: (naw mai) The Japanese name is mochigome. Round and opaque white, it's extremely sticky when cooked. This rice is used for stuffing, Chinese tamales or rice congee.

HOISIN SAUCE: (hoisin jeung) A deep brownish-red sauce made from soy beans, chili, garlic and vinegar. Very thick, spicy and sweet, it's used in seasoning spare ribs, roasting poultry or as a condiment, particularly with Muu Shu Pork or Peking Duck.

HOT BEAN SAUCE: See Bean sauce, Hot.

LEMON SAUCE (OR PASTE): (ming moan jeung) A thick jam-like amber sauce made from lemon and sugar. Used to season poultry or can be spread over buttered toast or biscuits for a unique and refreshing treat.

LILY BUDS - DRIED: (gum jum) Dried, 2-inch long flowers with a burnished gold color. They must be soaked and knotted to keep from falling apart during cooking. The small, hard lump at the end of each stem should be removed. Lily buds add a delicate, subtle flavor to poultry and often are used in vegetarian dishes.

MUSHROOMS - DRIED CHINESE: These come in several grades with the best called fa goo. They're thick and light in color on the underside, while the surfaces of the caps have many cracks. Edges are curled. When purchased by weight, you can be sure every fa goo is almost uniform in size. Fa goo should be saved for special dishes in which mushrooms are cooked whole. For other uses, buy less expensive grades since uniformity of size is inconsequential when they're to be sliced or diced. They must be soaked until soft. Stems are discarded and the caps cut according to directions.

MUSTARD GREENS: (guy choy) A jade green vegetable with a thick stem and wide, curved leaves. Slightly cool and bitter to the taste. Excellent for soup and a favorite pickling vegetable.

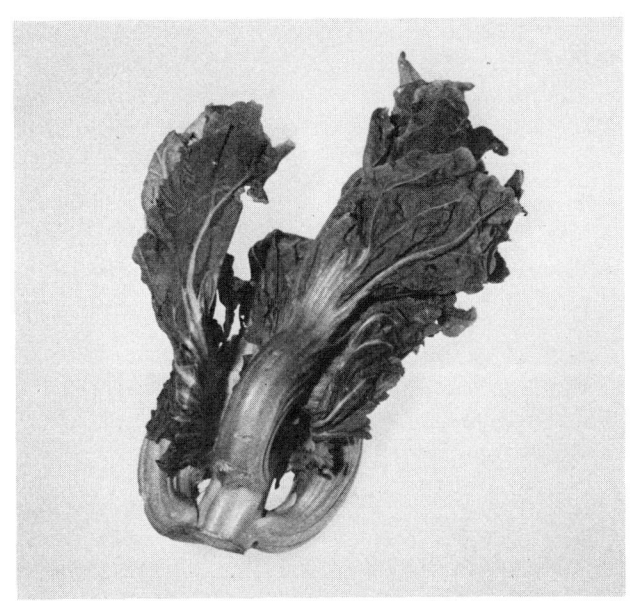

OYSTER SAUCE: (ho yow) A thick, rich, brown sauce made from oysters, but without a strong fishy odor. Its consistency is much like catsup and it's a favorite for seasoning meats. It's also used as a condiment.

PEPPER, SZECHWAN: An aromatic little pepper resembling the black peppercorn. It's used in meat and poultry dishes, and can be ground and mixed with salt for a seasoned dip.

PICKLED MUSTARD: See Turnips, Szechwan.

PLUM SAUCE: (sheung moy jeung) A thick, amber sauce with a pungent, spicy flavor made from plums, apricots, vinegar and sugar. This chutney-like sauce is used as one of the condiments with Peking Duck and often is called Duck Sauce. It can be refrigerated for months in a tightly covered jar.

PRESSED DUCK: (lop op) Golden colored ducks that have been dipped in oil, cured and flattened like a pancake. They're dried and hung against the wall in most stores. The bones are used for flavoring soups and the meat for flavoring pork, chicken, or rice in steamed dishes. Use sparingly.

RED DATES - DRIED: (hoan jo) Also known as jujube nuts, these are small, dried red fruit with wrinkled, glossy skins. They're used in soups or in steamed dishes to impart a subtle sweetness.

SAUSAGE, CHINESE: See Chinese Sausage.

SESAME OIL: (ma yau) A seasoning oil with a nut-like flavor, it's never used for cooking. One-half to 1 teaspoon sprinkled on top will do wonders for any dish.

SHRIMP - DRIED: (ha mai) Small, dried shrimp about ½-inch long. They should be soaked before using. They impart a delicate and subtle flavor.

SHRIMP PASTE: Ground, lavender colored shrimp that have been specially processed. Sold in jars, they have a strong, fishy odor. The Chinese like to use the paste for steamed or stir fried dishes.

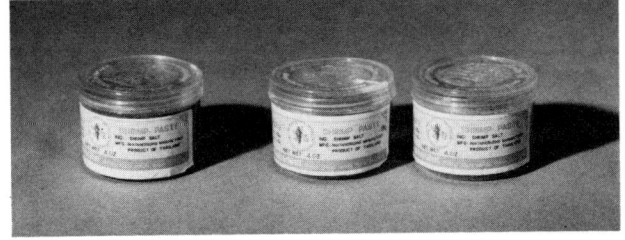

SOY SAUCE: (sang chau or see yau) A brown sauce made from soy beans, wheat, yeast and salt. The light or thin variety is lighter in color and density, and is used as a condiment in dishes such as sea food, where the color of the sauce shouldn't be apparent. The dark, thick or black variety is darker, thicker and has a full-bodied flavor. It's used when a deep brown color is desired.

SQUID - DRIED: Dried, flattened, and medium brown in color, they should be soaked overnight before using. Cut away all bony parts and re-soak for 15 minutes in baking soda. Cut into strips and score in a criss-cross fashion on one side so each piece will curl and open when stir fried.

STAR ANISE: (bot gok) A small cluster of dark brown, dry seeds shaped like an 8-pointed flower. it has a strong licorice flavor and is used in making soy sauce chicken, beef stew and in some soups.

SWEET CUCUMBERS: See Tea Melons.

SZECHWAN PEPPER: See Pepper, Szechwan.

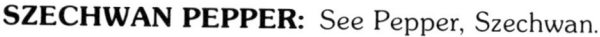

TANGERINE PEELS: (guaw pay) Dried, dark brown tangerine skin used in making soups, stews and cooking sauces. Sold by weight.

TEA MELON: (cha gwa) Also known as sweet cucumber, the amber vegetable is preserved in a syrup of honey and spices. The tiny squash is only 2 to 3 inches long, and has a sweet flavor and crunchy texture. Use chopped tea melons as a condiment for Joak, or slice them and steam with pork dishes. Available in cans. After the can is opened, remove contents to a jar and refrigerate. It'll keep for months.

THOUSAND YEAR OLD EGGS: (pay don) These eggs have been packed in a mixture of ashes, salt and lime. The egg white becomes firm, gelatinous and a deep shade of amber. The yolk takes on a dark green color and its consistency is much like a soft cheese. They're cut in wedges and served with pickled ginger as hors d'oeuvres or they can be used to garnish cold dishes.

TOFU: See Bean Cake.

TURNIP, CHINESE: (lo bak) Known as daikon in Japanese. Daikon often is more readily available then lo bak. This white vegetable looks like an overgrown horseradish and has a subtle flavor. It exudes a strong odor while cooking. Good for soups and stews.

TURNIP, SALTED: (choan choy) Brown, with a salty flavor, these turnips can be used sparingly in meat dishes in place of salt. They add flavor and textural interest.

TURNIP, SZECHWAN: (ja choy) Also known as pickled mustard, this hot, peppery, canned turnip is preserved with Szechwan pepper. Use in steamed dishes and hot and sour soup.

VINEGAR, RICE: (cho) Available in two colors: white or black. The white is much milder than its Western counterpart, and is used in Chinese salads and for seasoning light colored sauces. Black vinegar is used for dark colored sauces and braised dishes.

WATER CHESTNUTS: (ma tai) A bulb-like vegetable the size of a strawberry and grown in water. Fresh chestnuts are covered with mud and must be washed and peeled before eating. When sliced, they're good in stir frying or, when minced, for stuffings. They're also available in cans.

WET BEAN CURD: See Bean Curd - Wet.

WOOD EAR: (mook yee) Also known as wood fungus. A dry fungus similar to cloud ear fungus but thicker, tougher and crisper in texture. Must be soaked before using.

INDEX OF RECIPES

BEEF

Beef on a Stick, 49
Beef With Chives, 55
Chilled Beef Shank, 16
Ground Beef Casserole, 23
Mongolian Beef, 4
Oxtail and Chinese Turnip Stew, 20

POULTRY

Chicken and Chinese Sausage Casserole, 25
Chicken in Garlic and Ginger Sauce, 57
Chicken Wings with Mushrooms, 50
Curried Chicken with Vegetables, 19
Fragrant Crispy Chicken, 57
Kung Po Chicken, 2
Lemon Chicken, 67
Pan Pan Chicken, 11
Pineapple-Lemon Chicken, 64
Plum Sauce Chicken, 65
Red Ginger Chicken, 67
Roast Duck with Hoisin Sauce, 49
Smoke Chicken, 41
Smoke Game Hens L'Orange, 42
Smoke Tea Duck, 40
Spicy Chicken Salad, 14
Treasure Chicken, 56
Velvet Chicken with Spinach, 54

NOODLES AND RICE

Don Don Noodles, 82
Eight Jewels Rice, 25
Ja Jeing Mein, 81
Joak (Rice Congee), 26
Noodles with Shredded Pork and
    Pickled Mustard Greens, 83
Pork Lo Mein, 83

PORK

Anise Pork, 15
Banquet Pork, 50
Diced Pork in Lettuce Cups, 53
Muu Shu Pork, 78
Spicy Spareribs with Black Beans, 22
Steamed Pork with Pressed Duck, 32
Sweet and Sour Pork Shanghai, 63
Yu Hsiang Pork, 64

SEAFOOD

Abalone and Mushrooms in Oyster Sauce, 48
Braised Fish with Hot Bean Sauce, 9
Clams with Shrimp Paste, 34
Crab in Black Bean Sauce, 44
Crab in Peking Sauce, 43
Curried Crab, 44
Dried Squid with Chinese Long Beans, 33
Fish Fillet in Black Bean Sauce, 58

Fishballs with Bean Cakes and Mushrooms, 21
Ginger Crab with Sherry, 43
Salted Fish with Pork Patties, 30
Scallops with Snow Peas, 58
Sizzling Shrimp Platter, 70
Smoke Fish, 41
Spicy Shrimp, 2
Steamed Small Dried Fish, 29
Stuffed Phoenix Tail Prawns, 44
Sub Gum Fish, 45
Sweet and Sour Fish, 68

SOUPS

Dried Bok Choy Soup with Pressed Duck, 33
Hot and Sour Soup, 27
Sizzling Rice Soup, 26

VEGETABLES

Bean Cake Salad, 16
Braised Mushrooms in Oyster Sauce, 20
Chilled Braised Bamboo Shoots, 13
Chinese Cabbage in Cream Sauce, 60
Chinese Spinach Salad with
    Fresh Water Chestnuts, 13
Dry Cooked Green Beans, 30
Eggplant Szechwan, 7
Eggplant Szechwan with Pork, 7
Family Style Bean Cakes, 48
Pickled Vegetables, 36

Rainbow Salad, 13
Spicy Bean Cakes, 5
Spicy Cucumbers, 17
Spinach with Wet Bean Curd, 33
Stuffed Bean Cakes, 46
Stuffed Cucumber Rings, 60
Vegetarian Delight, 22
Yu Hsiang Eggplant, 8

WILD GAME

Breast of Mourning Dove in Hoisin Sauce, 75
Red Cook Wild Duck, 75
Spicy Venison, 74
Venison Stew, 73

MISCELLANEOUS

Ants Climbing the Tree, 8
Apple Crispies We-nat-chee, 71
Eggs in Soy Sauce, 36
Glazed Apples, 70
Golden Mountain Nuggets, 69
Hot Chili Oil with Garlic, 1
Lemon Paste, 35
Mongolian Fire Pot, 84
Onion Pancakes, 78
Peking Doilies, 80
Pot Stickers, 59
Red Cook Tripe, 16
Spicy Bean Thread with Minced Pork, 8
Thousand Year Old Eggs, 36

OTHER BOOKS BY TAYLOR & NG PRESS

PICNICS: by Joan Chatfield-Taylor. *Picnics* contains superb and delicious Mediterranean recipes, picnic plans and do-it-before time saving ideas for an outdoor meal event.

WOKCRAFT: by Charles & Violet Schafer. An authoritative and entertaining book on the art of Chinese wok cookery. Authentic, easy-to-follow recipes for beginners and professionals alike. Illustrated by Win Ng.

RICECRAFT: Margaret Gin delves into the fact, fiction and fancy of rice. A collection of inventive recipes, from simple to exotic, takes full advantage of the international versitility of rice. Fanciful illustrations by Win Ng.

TEACRAFT: Charles and Violet Schafer's tea treasury of romance, rituals & recipes explores tea's origin, its extensive variety and multiplicity of uses. A test and taste chapter guides you to a true connoisseurship. Illustrated by Win Ng.

HERBCRAFT: Violet Schafer unveils the mysteries, origins, history, growing and storing conditions of 26 herbs in a delightful Win Ng illustrated handbook. *Herbcraft* also charts gardens and records healthful recipes.

COFFEE: The story behind your morning cup - exploring the history and lore of coffee, grinding and brewing hints, what to brew it in, etc. Charles and Violet Schafer also cite a delicious collection of companion food recipes. Photo-illustrated.

CHINESE VILLAGE COOKBOOK: Celebrated Rhoda Yee tells you all about the wok and Chinese cookery, with colorful narratives on everyday life in a Chinese village. Excellent easy-to-prepare recipes and a helpful stirfrying chart.

DIM SUM: Rhoda Yee's second book reveals the savory secrets of Dim Sum, the traditional Chinese tea lunch and helps you prepare it in your home. Techniques and end results are photo-documented.

GREAT ASIA STEAMBOOK: Irene Wong's practical guide to steam cooking techniques and recipes from all Asian countries. A delicious blending of an international cuisine that is both nutritious and energy-saving. Photo-illustrated.

NO PRESSURE STEAM COOKING: Robert Zinkhon's delightful guide to a wide range of steamed foods from meats to vegetables, breads to desserts. Steam cooking's energy-saving & nutritional qualities are matched with time-saving techniques.

DOG & CAT GOOD FOOD BOOK: Author Terri McGuinnis, veterinarian and pet expert, unravels the myths about what foods are nutritionally beneficial to pets of all ages; lists charts to guide and recipes that work. Illustrated by Margaret Choi.